# TEACHER'S PET PUBLICATIONS

PUZZLE PACK
for
The Hound of the Baskervilles

based on the book by
Sir Arthur Conan Doyle

Written by
William T. Collins

© 2005 Teacher's Pet Publications
All Rights Reserved

The materials in this packet are copyrighted
by Teacher's Pet Publications, Inc.

These pages may be duplicated by the purchaser
for use in the purchaser's own classroom.

Copying any of these materials and distributing them
for any other purpose is a violation of the copyright laws.

© 2005 Teacher's Pet Publications, Inc.
www.tpet.com

INTRODUCTION
If you already own the LitPlan for this title, this Puzzle Pack will refresh your Unit Resource Materials and Vocabulary Resource Materials sections plus give you additional materials you can substitute into the tests. If you do not already have a complete LitPlan, these pages will give you some supplemental materials to use with your own plan. There are two main groups of materials: one set for unit words (such as characters' names, symbols, places, etc.) and one set for vocabulary words associated with the book.

WORD LIST
There is a word list for both the unit words and the vocabulary words. These lists show you which words are being used in the materials and the clues or definitions being used for those words. You may want to give students a word list with clues/definitions to help them, or you may want students to only have a word list (without clues/definitions) if you want them to work a little harder. Both are available for duplication. The word lists can also be your "calling key" for the bingo games.

FILL IN THE BLANK AND MATCHING
There are 4 each of the fill in the blank and matching worksheets for both the unit and vocabulary words. These pages can be used either as extra worksheets for students or as objective parts of a unit test. They can be done individually if students need extra help or as a whole class activity to review the material covered.

MAGIC SQUARES
The magic squares not only reinforce the material covered but also work on reasoning and math skills. Many teachers have told us that their students really enjoy doing these!

WORD SEARCH PUZZLES
The word search words go in all directions, as indicated on your answer keys. Two of the word search puzzles have the clues listed rather than the words. This makes the puzzle a little more difficult, but it reinforces the material better. Two word search puzzles have words only for students who find the clue puzzles too difficult.

CROSSWORD PUZZLES
Both unit and vocabulary word sections have 4 crossword puzzles.

BINGO CARDS
There are 32 individual bingo cards for the unit words and 32 individual bingo cards for the vocabulary words. You can use your word list as a "call list," calling the words at random and marking them off of your list as you go, or you could use the flash cards by cutting them apart and drawing the words at random from a hat (or box or whatever). To make a better review, you might ask for the definition and spelling of each word as you call it out–or you could call out the definitions and have students tell you the words they need to look for on the puzzle.

JUGGLE LETTERS
The vocabulary juggle letter game is intended to help students learn the spellings of the words. One sheet has the definitions listed on it as an extra help for students who need it or to reinforce the definitions if you choose to do so.

FLASH CARDS
We've included a set of vocabulary flash cards you can duplicate, cut, and fold for your students. Some teachers make a few sets for general use by the class; others make a set for each student. Some teachers duplicate them for each student and have the students cut & fold their own. You can cut out just the words and put them in a hat, have each student pick out one word and write the definition and a sentence for that word. Students then swap words and papers, with the next student adding a sentence of his own under the last one. You can have students swap as many times as you like. Each time the student will read the sentences written prior to his own and then add a sentence. You can cut out the words and definitions separately and play "I Have; Who Has?" Each student in the room draws a word and definition. The first student says, "I have (the name of the word). Who has the definition?" The student with the definition reads it then says, "I have (the name of the vocabulary word she has). Who has the definition?" The round continues until all words and definitions have been given.

Hound of the Baskervilles Word List

No.	Word	Clue/Definition
1.	BARRYMORE	Servant to Charles and Henry
2.	BASKERVILLES	Hound of the ___
3.	BERYL	Mrs. Stapleton
4.	CAB	The spy rode in one.
5.	CARTWRIGHT	Holmes's boy helper
6.	CHARLES	Died of heart failure
7.	CIGAR	Sir Charles smoked one
8.	COOMB	Laura lived there: ___ Tracey
9.	DETECTIVE	Holmes or Watson, for example
10.	DOG	Spaniel or hound, for example
11.	DOYLE	Sir Arthur Conan ___
12.	ENGLAND	London's country
13.	ESTATE	The whole of one's possessions
14.	EVIDENCE	Clues; Sherlock gathers this
15.	FOOTPRINT	The hound left this 20 feet from Charles
16.	FRANKLAND	Laura's father
17.	GATE	CB waited to meet LL there
18.	GRIMPEN	Mire
19.	HEART	Sir Charles had a bad one
20.	HENRY	Charles's heir
21.	HOLMES	Chief detective on the Baskerville case
22.	HOWL	Sound of the hound
23.	HUGO	He sold out to the powers of evil
24.	INHERIT	Receive from a will
25.	INTO	Stapleton fell ___ the mire.
26.	KIN	Relatives
27.	LYONS	Laura
28.	MAN	___ on the Tor
29.	MEET	To be introduced to someone
30.	MERRIPIT	Stapleton's house
31.	MOON	Nature's night light
32.	MOOR	Bad luck place for the Baskervilles
33.	MORTIMER	Doctor to Charles
34.	MOTIVE	Reason for behavior
35.	NORTHUMBERLAND	Hotel
36.	PERKINS	Groom
37.	REGENT	SH saw the spy on this street
38.	REPORT	Watson sent one to Holmes often
39.	SELDEN	Convict
40.	SHERLOCK	___ Holmes
41.	SOB	Watson heard Mrs. B. doing this.
42.	STAPLETON	Tried to kill Henry
43.	STONE	Kind of huts on the hill
44.	TOR	The man on the ___
45.	WALKING	SH examined Mortimer's ___ stick
46.	WATSON	Holmes's assistant
47.	WOO	Court towards marriage
48.	YEWALLEY	Walkway where Charles died

Hound of the Baskervilles Fill In The Blanks 1

_____ 1. Bad luck place for the Baskervilles

_____ 2. Hound of the ___

_____ 3. Holmes's boy helper

_____ 4. The man on the ___

_____ 5. Died of heart failure

_____ 6. Doctor to Charles

_____ 7. CB waited to meet LL there

_____ 8. Clues; Sherlock gathers this

_____ 9. Laura

_____ 10. Receive from a will

_____ 11. ___ Holmes

_____ 12. Charles's heir

_____ 13. Sir Charles had a bad one

_____ 14. SH examined Mortimer's ____ stick

_____ 15. Stapleton's house

_____ 16. Kind of huts on the hill

_____ 17. Sir Arthur Conan ___

_____ 18. Holmes's assistant

_____ 19. Stapleton fell ___ the mire.

_____ 20. Laura lived there: ___ Tracey

Hound of the Baskervilles Fill In The Blanks 1 Answer Key

MOOR	1. Bad luck place for the Baskervilles
BASKERVILLES	2. Hound of the ___
CARTWRIGHT	3. Holmes's boy helper
TOR	4. The man on the ___
CHARLES	5. Died of heart failure
MORTIMER	6. Doctor to Charles
GATE	7. CB waited to meet LL there
EVIDENCE	8. Clues; Sherlock gathers this
LYONS	9. Laura
INHERIT	10. Receive from a will
SHERLOCK	11. ___ Holmes
HENRY	12. Charles's heir
HEART	13. Sir Charles had a bad one
WALKING	14. SH examined Mortimer's ____ stick
MERRIPIT	15. Stapleton's house
STONE	16. Kind of huts on the hill
DOYLE	17. Sir Arthur Conan ___
WATSON	18. Holmes's assistant
INTO	19. Stapleton fell ___ the mire.
COOMB	20. Laura lived there: ___ Tracey

Hound of the Baskervilles Fill In The Blanks 2

_____ 1. Sir Charles smoked one

_____ 2. To be introduced to someone

_____ 3. Mrs. Stapleton

_____ 4. Charles's heir

_____ 5. Reason for behavior

_____ 6. Holmes's assistant

_____ 7. The hound left this 20 feet from Charles

_____ 8. The spy rode in one.

_____ 9. Hotel

_____ 10. Kind of huts on the hill

_____ 11. Laura

_____ 12. The whole of one's possessions

_____ 13. ___ Holmes

_____ 14. Tried to kill Henry

_____ 15. Sound of the hound

_____ 16. Sir Arthur Conan ___

_____ 17. Court towards marriage

_____ 18. Holmes's boy helper

_____ 19. Doctor to Charles

_____ 20. He sold out to the powers of evil

Hound of the Baskervilles Fill In The Blanks 2 Answer Key

Answer	Clue
CIGAR	1. Sir Charles smoked one
MEET	2. To be introduced to someone
BERYL	3. Mrs. Stapleton
HENRY	4. Charles's heir
MOTIVE	5. Reason for behavior
WATSON	6. Holmes's assistant
FOOTPRINT	7. The hound left this 20 feet from Charles
CAB	8. The spy rode in one.
NORTHUMBERLAND	9. Hotel
STONE	10. Kind of huts on the hill
LYONS	11. Laura
ESTATE	12. The whole of one's possessions
SHERLOCK	13. ___ Holmes
STAPLETON	14. Tried to kill Henry
HOWL	15. Sound of the hound
DOYLE	16. Sir Arthur Conan ___
WOO	17. Court towards marriage
CARTWRIGHT	18. Holmes's boy helper
MORTIMER	19. Doctor to Charles
HUGO	20. He sold out to the powers of evil

Hound of the Baskervilles Fill In The Blanks 3

1. Mrs. Stapleton
2. Sir Charles had a bad one
3. Tried to kill Henry
4. Sir Charles smoked one
5. Bad luck place for the Baskervilles
6. Doctor to Charles
7. The spy rode in one.
8. Chief detective on the Baskerville case
9. ___ on the Tor
10. Holmes's boy helper
11. Kind of huts on the hill
12. Holmes or Watson, for example
13. Court towards marriage
14. Laura's father
15. SH examined Mortimer's ____ stick
16. Watson sent one to Holmes often
17. Spaniel or hound, for example
18. Mire
19. Walkway where Charles died
20. Receive from a will

Hound of the Baskervilles Fill In The Blanks 3 Answer Key

BERYL	1. Mrs. Stapleton
HEART	2. Sir Charles had a bad one
STAPLETON	3. Tried to kill Henry
CIGAR	4. Sir Charles smoked one
MOOR	5. Bad luck place for the Baskervilles
MORTIMER	6. Doctor to Charles
CAB	7. The spy rode in one.
HOLMES	8. Chief detective on the Baskerville case
MAN	9. ___ on the Tor
CARTWRIGHT	10. Holmes's boy helper
STONE	11. Kind of huts on the hill
DETECTIVE	12. Holmes or Watson, for example
WOO	13. Court towards marriage
FRANKLAND	14. Laura's father
WALKING	15. SH examined Mortimer's ____ stick
REPORT	16. Watson sent one to Holmes often
DOG	17. Spaniel or hound, for example
GRIMPEN	18. Mire
YEWALLEY	19. Walkway where Charles died
INHERIT	20. Receive from a will

Hound of the Baskervilles Fill In The Blanks 4

_____   1. Spaniel or hound, for example

_____   2. Holmes's assistant

_____   3. Laura

_____   4. To be introduced to someone

_____   5. Watson sent one to Holmes often

_____   6. SH examined Mortimer's ____ stick

_____   7. Servant to Charles and Henry

_____   8. The man on the ___

_____   9. The spy rode in one.

_____   10. Receive from a will

_____   11. He sold out to the powers of evil

_____   12. Stapleton fell ___ the mire.

_____   13. Clues; Sherlock gathers this

_____   14. Groom

_____   15. Court towards marriage

_____   16. Holmes or Watson, for example

_____   17. Sir Charles had a bad one

_____   18. Died of heart failure

_____   19. Doctor to Charles

_____   20. Mrs. Stapleton

Hound of the Baskervilles Fill In The Blanks 4 Answer Key

Answer	Clue
DOG	1. Spaniel or hound, for example
WATSON	2. Holmes's assistant
LYONS	3. Laura
MEET	4. To be introduced to someone
REPORT	5. Watson sent one to Holmes often
WALKING	6. SH examined Mortimer's ____ stick
BARRYMORE	7. Servant to Charles and Henry
TOR	8. The man on the ___
CAB	9. The spy rode in one.
INHERIT	10. Receive from a will
HUGO	11. He sold out to the powers of evil
INTO	12. Stapleton fell ___ the mire.
EVIDENCE	13. Clues; Sherlock gathers this
PERKINS	14. Groom
WOO	15. Court towards marriage
DETECTIVE	16. Holmes or Watson, for example
HEART	17. Sir Charles had a bad one
CHARLES	18. Died of heart failure
MORTIMER	19. Doctor to Charles
BERYL	20. Mrs. Stapleton

Hound of the Baskervilles Matching 1

___ 1. SHERLOCK   A. ___ Holmes
___ 2. INTO   B. To be introduced to someone
___ 3. COOMB   C. London's country
___ 4. INHERIT   D. Sir Charles had a bad one
___ 5. REPORT   E. Walkway where Charles died
___ 6. DOYLE   F. Watson sent one to Holmes often
___ 7. CIGAR   G. Nature's night light
___ 8. MEET   H. The hound left this 20 feet from Charles
___ 9. ENGLAND   I. Sir Arthur Conan ___
___ 10. GATE   J. Reason for behavior
___ 11. MORTIMER   K. Doctor to Charles
___ 12. PERKINS   L. Hotel
___ 13. YEWALLEY   M. Mire
___ 14. REGENT   N. Laura
___ 15. WOO   O. Laura lived there: ___ Tracey
___ 16. HEART   P. CB waited to meet LL there
___ 17. GRIMPEN   Q. Groom
___ 18. LYONS   R. Sir Charles smoked one
___ 19. MOON   S. The whole of one's possessions
___ 20. ESTATE   T. SH saw the spy on this street
___ 21. FOOTPRINT   U. Bad luck place for the Baskervilles
___ 22. MOTIVE   V. Receive from a will
___ 23. MOOR   W. Stapleton fell ___ the mire.
___ 24. NORTHUMBERLAND   X. Convict
___ 25. SELDEN   Y. Court towards marriage

Hound of the Baskervilles Matching 1 Answer Key

A - 1. SHERLOCK	A. ___ Holmes
W - 2. INTO	B. To be introduced to someone
O - 3. COOMB	C. London's country
V - 4. INHERIT	D. Sir Charles had a bad one
F - 5. REPORT	E. Walkway where Charles died
I - 6. DOYLE	F. Watson sent one to Holmes often
R - 7. CIGAR	G. Nature's night light
B - 8. MEET	H. The hound left this 20 feet from Charles
C - 9. ENGLAND	I. Sir Arthur Conan ___
P - 10. GATE	J. Reason for behavior
K - 11. MORTIMER	K. Doctor to Charles
Q - 12. PERKINS	L. Hotel
E - 13. YEWALLEY	M. Mire
T - 14. REGENT	N. Laura
Y - 15. WOO	O. Laura lived there: ___ Tracey
D - 16. HEART	P. CB waited to meet LL there
M - 17. GRIMPEN	Q. Groom
N - 18. LYONS	R. Sir Charles smoked one
G - 19. MOON	S. The whole of one's possessions
S - 20. ESTATE	T. SH saw the spy on this street
H - 21. FOOTPRINT	U. Bad luck place for the Baskervilles
J - 22. MOTIVE	V. Receive from a will
U - 23. MOOR	W. Stapleton fell ___ the mire.
L - 24. NORTHUMBERLAND	X. Convict
X - 25. SELDEN	Y. Court towards marriage

Copyrighted

Hound of the Baskervilles Matching 2

___ 1. WOO A. Holmes or Watson, for example
___ 2. BARRYMORE B. Court towards marriage
___ 3. FRANKLAND C. Servant to Charles and Henry
___ 4. KIN D. He sold out to the powers of evil
___ 5. MOTIVE E. Stapleton fell ___ the mire.
___ 6. MORTIMER F. Bad luck place for the Baskervilles
___ 7. DOYLE G. Nature's night light
___ 8. HOLMES H. Receive from a will
___ 9. HEART I. Reason for behavior
___10. REPORT J. The man on the ___
___11. DETECTIVE K. SH saw the spy on this street
___12. YEWALLEY L. Stapleton's house
___13. HUGO M. Kind of huts on the hill
___14. INHERIT N. Doctor to Charles
___15. TOR O. Holmes's boy helper
___16. MOON P. Walkway where Charles died
___17. REGENT Q. Sir Arthur Conan ___
___18. MOOR R. Watson sent one to Holmes often
___19. STONE S. To be introduced to someone
___20. DOG T. Spaniel or hound, for example
___21. INTO U. Relatives
___22. MEET V. Holmes's assistant
___23. CARTWRIGHT W. Chief detective on the Baskerville case
___24. WATSON X. Sir Charles had a bad one
___25. MERRIPIT Y. Laura's father

Hound of the Baskervilles Matching 2 Answer Key

B - 1. WOO	A.	Holmes or Watson, for example
C - 2. BARRYMORE	B.	Court towards marriage
Y - 3. FRANKLAND	C.	Servant to Charles and Henry
U - 4. KIN	D.	He sold out to the powers of evil
I - 5. MOTIVE	E.	Stapleton fell ___ the mire.
N - 6. MORTIMER	F.	Bad luck place for the Baskervilles
Q - 7. DOYLE	G.	Nature's night light
W - 8. HOLMES	H.	Receive from a will
X - 9. HEART	I.	Reason for behavior
R -10. REPORT	J.	The man on the ___
A -11. DETECTIVE	K.	SH saw the spy on this street
P -12. YEWALLEY	L.	Stapleton's house
D -13. HUGO	M.	Kind of huts on the hill
H -14. INHERIT	N.	Doctor to Charles
J -15. TOR	O.	Holmes's boy helper
G -16. MOON	P.	Walkway where Charles died
K -17. REGENT	Q.	Sir Arthur Conan ___
F -18. MOOR	R.	Watson sent one to Holmes often
M -19. STONE	S.	To be introduced to someone
T -20. DOG	T.	Spaniel or hound, for example
E -21. INTO	U.	Relatives
S -22. MEET	V.	Holmes's assistant
O -23. CARTWRIGHT	W.	Chief detective on the Baskerville case
V -24. WATSON	X.	Sir Charles had a bad one
L -25. MERRIPIT	Y.	Laura's father

Copyrighted

Hound of the Baskervilles Matching 3

___ 1. MOOR   A. Reason for behavior
___ 2. FRANKLAND   B. Stapleton's house
___ 3. MOTIVE   C. He sold out to the powers of evil
___ 4. INTO   D. Laura
___ 5. MEET   E. Bad luck place for the Baskervilles
___ 6. SELDEN   F. Relatives
___ 7. TOR   G. Servant to Charles and Henry
___ 8. PERKINS   H. Convict
___ 9. WOO   I. Charles's heir
___10. GATE   J. Holmes or Watson, for example
___11. EVIDENCE   K. The man on the ___
___12. FOOTPRINT   L. Court towards marriage
___13. SOB   M. To be introduced to someone
___14. DETECTIVE   N. Holmes's boy helper
___15. LYONS   O. CB waited to meet LL there
___16. CARTWRIGHT   P. Clues; Sherlock gathers this
___17. WATSON   Q. Groom
___18. MOON   R. The hound left this 20 feet from Charles
___19. BARRYMORE   S. ___ on the Tor
___20. YEWALLEY   T. Stapleton fell ___ the mire.
___21. KIN   U. Walkway where Charles died
___22. MERRIPIT   V. Holmes's assistant
___23. MAN   W. Laura's father
___24. HUGO   X. Nature's night light
___25. HENRY   Y. Watson heard Mrs. B. doing this.

Hound of the Baskervilles Matching 3 Answer Key

E - 1.	MOOR	A. Reason for behavior
W - 2.	FRANKLAND	B. Stapleton's house
A - 3.	MOTIVE	C. He sold out to the powers of evil
T - 4.	INTO	D. Laura
M - 5.	MEET	E. Bad luck place for the Baskervilles
H - 6.	SELDEN	F. Relatives
K - 7.	TOR	G. Servant to Charles and Henry
Q - 8.	PERKINS	H. Convict
L - 9.	WOO	I. Charles's heir
O - 10.	GATE	J. Holmes or Watson, for example
P - 11.	EVIDENCE	K. The man on the ___
R - 12.	FOOTPRINT	L. Court towards marriage
Y - 13.	SOB	M. To be introduced to someone
J - 14.	DETECTIVE	N. Holmes's boy helper
D - 15.	LYONS	O. CB waited to meet LL there
N - 16.	CARTWRIGHT	P. Clues; Sherlock gathers this
V - 17.	WATSON	Q. Groom
X - 18.	MOON	R. The hound left this 20 feet from Charles
G - 19.	BARRYMORE	S. ___ on the Tor
U - 20.	YEWALLEY	T. Stapleton fell ___ the mire.
F - 21.	KIN	U. Walkway where Charles died
B - 22.	MERRIPIT	V. Holmes's assistant
S - 23.	MAN	W. Laura's father
C - 24.	HUGO	X. Nature's night light
I - 25.	HENRY	Y. Watson heard Mrs. B. doing this.

Hound of the Baskervilles Matching 4

___ 1. CHARLES   A. Court towards marriage
___ 2. ESTATE   B. Watson heard Mrs. B. doing this.
___ 3. FOOTPRINT   C. Sir Charles had a bad one
___ 4. BARRYMORE   D. Died of heart failure
___ 5. KIN   E. He sold out to the powers of evil
___ 6. STAPLETON   F. Groom
___ 7. PERKINS   G. Spaniel or hound, for example
___ 8. REPORT   H. Convict
___ 9. BERYL   I. Laura's father
___10. SOB   J. Holmes's boy helper
___11. ENGLAND   K. Servant to Charles and Henry
___12. INHERIT   L. Relatives
___13. DOYLE   M. Kind of huts on the hill
___14. HUGO   N. SH saw the spy on this street
___15. DOG   O. Bad luck place for the Baskervilles
___16. STONE   P. Tried to kill Henry
___17. LYONS   Q. Receive from a will
___18. SELDEN   R. The hound left this 20 feet from Charles
___19. MOOR   S. Sound of the hound
___20. HOWL   T. Laura
___21. HEART   U. Watson sent one to Holmes often
___22. WOO   V. London's country
___23. CARTWRIGHT   W. Mrs. Stapleton
___24. REGENT   X. The whole of one's possessions
___25. FRANKLAND   Y. Sir Arthur Conan ___

Hound of the Baskervilles Matching 4 Answer Key

D - 1. CHARLES	A. Court towards marriage
X - 2. ESTATE	B. Watson heard Mrs. B. doing this.
R - 3. FOOTPRINT	C. Sir Charles had a bad one
K - 4. BARRYMORE	D. Died of heart failure
L - 5. KIN	E. He sold out to the powers of evil
P - 6. STAPLETON	F. Groom
F - 7. PERKINS	G. Spaniel or hound, for example
U - 8. REPORT	H. Convict
W - 9. BERYL	I. Laura's father
B - 10. SOB	J. Holmes's boy helper
V - 11. ENGLAND	K. Servant to Charles and Henry
Q - 12. INHERIT	L. Relatives
Y - 13. DOYLE	M. Kind of huts on the hill
E - 14. HUGO	N. SH saw the spy on this street
G - 15. DOG	O. Bad luck place for the Baskervilles
M - 16. STONE	P. Tried to kill Henry
T - 17. LYONS	Q. Receive from a will
H - 18. SELDEN	R. The hound left this 20 feet from Charles
O - 19. MOOR	S. Sound of the hound
S - 20. HOWL	T. Laura
C - 21. HEART	U. Watson sent one to Holmes often
A - 22. WOO	V. London's country
J - 23. CARTWRIGHT	W. Mrs. Stapleton
N - 24. REGENT	X. The whole of one's possessions
I - 25. FRANKLAND	Y. Sir Arthur Conan ___

Hound of the Baskervilles Magic Squares 1

Match the definition with the vocabulary word. Put your answers in the magic squares below. When your answers are correct, all columns and rows will add to the same number.

A. SHERLOCK
B. DOG
C. KIN
D. STAPLETON
E. WALKING
F. MAN
G. HENRY
H. NORTHUMBERLAND
I. GRIMPEN
J. DOYLE
K. INHERIT
L. HOLMES
M. WATSON
N. PERKINS
O. LYONS
P. GATE

1. Laura
2. Sir Arthur Conan ___
3. Hotel
4. ___ Holmes
5. Tried to kill Henry
6. SH examined Mortimer's ____ stick
7. Receive from a will
8. Groom
9. ___ on the Tor
10. Relatives
11. Holmes's assistant
12. Chief detective on the Baskerville case
13. Mire
14. CB waited to meet LL there
15. Spaniel or hound, for example
16. Charles's heir

A= 4	B= 15	C= 10	D= 5
E= 6	F= 9	G= 16	H= 3
I= 13	J= 2	K= 7	L= 12
M= 11	N= 8	O= 1	P= 14

Hound of the Baskervilles Magic Squares 1 Answer Key

Match the definition with the vocabulary word. Put your answers in the magic squares below. When your answers are correct, all columns and rows will add to the same number.

A. SHERLOCK
B. DOG
C. KIN
D. STAPLETON
E. WALKING
F. MAN

G. HENRY
H. NORTHUMBERLAND
I. GRIMPEN
J. DOYLE
K. INHERIT
L. HOLMES

M. WATSON
N. PERKINS
O. LYONS
P. GATE

1. Laura
2. Sir Arthur Conan ___
3. Hotel
4. ___ Holmes
5. Tried to kill Henry
6. SH examined Mortimer's ___ stick
7. Receive from a will
8. Groom
9. ___ on the Tor
10. Relatives
11. Holmes's assistant
12. Chief detective on the Baskerville case
13. Mire
14. CB waited to meet LL there
15. Spaniel or hound, for example
16. Charles's heir

A=4	B=15	C=10	D=5
E=6	F=9	G=16	H=3
I=13	J=2	K=7	L=12
M=11	N=8	O=1	P=14

Hound of the Baskervilles Magic Squares 2

Match the definition with the vocabulary word. Put your answers in the magic squares below. When your answers are correct, all columns and rows will add to the same number.

A. MORTIMER
B. REPORT
C. YEWALLEY
D. INTO
E. SOB
F. HENRY
G. LYONS
H. WATSON
I. TOR
J. DETECTIVE
K. SHERLOCK
L. MERRIPIT
M. DOG
N. COOMB
O. HOLMES
P. GRIMPEN

1. Watson sent one to Holmes often
2. Laura
3. ___ Holmes
4. Laura lived there: ___ Tracey
5. Spaniel or hound, for example
6. Stapleton's house
7. Holmes's assistant
8. Doctor to Charles
9. Mire
10. The man on the ___
11. Watson heard Mrs. B. doing this.
12. Stapleton fell ___ the mire.
13. Walkway where Charles died
14. Charles's heir
15. Holmes or Watson, for example
16. Chief detective on the Baskerville case

A=	B=	C=	D=
E=	F=	G=	H=
I=	J=	K=	L=
M=	N=	O=	P=

23
Copyrighted

Hound of the Baskervilles Magic Squares 2 Answer Key

Match the definition with the vocabulary word. Put your answers in the magic squares below. When your answers are correct, all columns and rows will add to the same number.

A. MORTIMER
B. REPORT
C. YEWALLEY
D. INTO
E. SOB
F. HENRY
G. LYONS
H. WATSON
I. TOR
J. DETECTIVE
K. SHERLOCK
L. MERRIPIT
M. DOG
N. COOMB
O. HOLMES
P. GRIMPEN

1. Watson sent one to Holmes often
2. Laura
3. ___ Holmes
4. Laura lived there: ___ Tracey
5. Spaniel or hound, for example
6. Stapleton's house
7. Holmes's assistant
8. Doctor to Charles
9. Mire
10. The man on the ___
11. Watson heard Mrs. B. doing this.
12. Stapleton fell ___ the mire.
13. Walkway where Charles died
14. Charles's heir
15. Holmes or Watson, for example
16. Chief detective on the Baskerville case

A=8	B=1	C=13	D=12
E=11	F=14	G=2	H=7
I=10	J=15	K=3	L=6
M=5	N=4	O=16	P=9

Hound of the Baskervilles Magic Squares 3

Match the definition with the vocabulary word. Put your answers in the magic squares below. When your answers are correct, all columns and rows will add to the same number.

A. CIGAR
B. CARTWRIGHT
C. CAB
D. LYONS
E. STAPLETON
F. NORTHUMBERLAND
G. BASKERVILLES
H. MAN
I. HOLMES
J. DETECTIVE
K. BERYL
L. SELDEN
M. MORTIMER
N. PERKINS
O. WATSON
P. FRANKLAND

1. Hotel
2. Chief detective on the Baskerville case
3. Holmes's assistant
4. Laura
5. Doctor to Charles
6. Holmes's boy helper
7. ___ on the Tor
8. Mrs. Stapleton
9. The spy rode in one.
10. Laura's father
11. Holmes or Watson, for example
12. Tried to kill Henry
13. Convict
14. Hound of the ___
15. Sir Charles smoked one
16. Groom

A= 15	B= 6	C= 9	D= 4
E= 12	F= 1	G= 14	H= 7
I= 2	J= 11	K= 8	L= 13
M= 5	N= 16	O= 3	P= 10

Hound of the Baskervilles Magic Squares 3 Answer Key

Match the definition with the vocabulary word. Put your answers in the magic squares below. When your answers are correct, all columns and rows will add to the same number.

A. CIGAR
B. CARTWRIGHT
C. CAB
D. LYONS
E. STAPLETON
F. NORTHUMBERLAND
G. BASKERVILLES
H. MAN
I. HOLMES
J. DETECTIVE
K. BERYL
L. SELDEN
M. MORTIMER
N. PERKINS
O. WATSON
P. FRANKLAND

1. Hotel
2. Chief detective on the Baskerville case
3. Holmes's assistant
4. Laura
5. Doctor to Charles
6. Holmes's boy helper
7. ___ on the Tor
8. Mrs. Stapleton
9. The spy rode in one.
10. Laura's father
11. Holmes or Watson, for example
12. Tried to kill Henry
13. Convict
14. Hound of the ___
15. Sir Charles smoked one
16. Groom

A=15	B=6	C=9	D=4
E=12	F=1	G=14	H=7
I=2	J=11	K=8	L=13
M=5	N=16	O=3	P=10

Hound of the Baskervilles Magic Squares 4

Match the definition with the vocabulary word. Put your answers in the magic squares below. When your answers are correct, all columns and rows will add to the same number.

A. HEART
B. EVIDENCE
C. MEET
D. HOWL
E. SELDEN
F. MAN
G. REPORT
H. CAB
I. SOB
J. MOON
K. COOMB
L. MOOR
M. TOR
N. DOG
O. GATE
P. PERKINS

1. The man on the ___
2. ___ on the Tor
3. The spy rode in one.
4. CB waited to meet LL there
5. Bad luck place for the Baskervilles
6. To be introduced to someone
7. Sir Charles had a bad one
8. Nature's night light
9. Laura lived there: ___ Tracey
10. Sound of the hound
11. Clues; Sherlock gathers this
12. Watson heard Mrs. B. doing this.
13. Spaniel or hound, for example
14. Convict
15. Watson sent one to Holmes often
16. Groom

A=	B=	C=	D=
E=	F=	G=	H=
I=	J=	K=	L=
M=	N=	O=	P=

Hound of the Baskervilles Magic Squares 4 Answer Key

Match the definition with the vocabulary word. Put your answers in the magic squares below. When your answers are correct, all columns and rows will add to the same number.

A. HEART
B. EVIDENCE
C. MEET
D. HOWL
E. SELDEN
F. MAN
G. REPORT
H. CAB
I. SOB
J. MOON
K. COOMB
L. MOOR
M. TOR
N. DOG
O. GATE
P. PERKINS

1. The man on the ___
2. ___ on the Tor
3. The spy rode in one.
4. CB waited to meet LL there
5. Bad luck place for the Baskervilles
6. To be introduced to someone
7. Sir Charles had a bad one
8. Nature's night light
9. Laura lived there: ___ Tracey
10. Sound of the hound
11. Clues; Sherlock gathers this
12. Watson heard Mrs. B. doing this.
13. Spaniel or hound, for example
14. Convict
15. Watson sent one to Holmes often
16. Groom

A=7	B=11	C=6	D=10
E=14	F=2	G=15	H=3
I=12	J=8	K=9	L=5
M=1	N=13	O=4	P=16

Hound of the Baskervilles Word Search 1

Words are placed backwards, forward, diagonally, up and down. Clues listed below can help you find the words. Circle the hidden vocabulary words in the maze.

```
C K P D E G V Y G A T E N O S T A W B W S
I L S P M N E V P Y W L N N B G M T A M F
G X F W Y L G M W G L P O P X H W J R V F
A K B J L Y C L L P J Y T F P N A C R E J
R Q T A W T W S A V L M E C E D L K Y V F
Y X W R V M P H B N Q T L W V G K G M I F
F E X Y T P E E T Z D I P B I X I E O T Z
Y S F O O T P R I N T R A S D C N S R C C
G S M X F V J L R P Q E T S E D G T E E V
K R C D Q P R O T I Y H S D N L L A S T T
I F I A F D W C K T P N D H C R D T R E H
N V S M B A S K E R V I L L E S R E E D G
Y K F H P B P G H L K B T P E N G M N C I
V B Q Y E E S T M S Q C O M W E R A Y O R
M H S L G A N C C O H R L Y N G L Y G O W
D Z Y R T O R R J A T O L T G K B N A M T
X O O V M I J T R S H I Z C N O M E P B R
D O B V N L H L V R V D V A S D O O R V A
M O R T I M E R S N I K R E P H O W L Y C
S T O N E S H U G O F F G T C W N G G G L
```

Bad luck place for the Baskervilles (4)
CB waited to meet LL there (4)
Charles's heir (5)
Chief detective on the Baskerville case (6)
Clues; Sherlock gathers this (8)
Convict (6)
Court towards marriage (3)
Died of heart failure (7)
Doctor to Charles (8)
Groom (7)
He sold out to the powers of evil (4)
Holmes or Watson, for example (9)
Holmes's assistant (6)
Holmes's boy helper (10)
Hound of the ___ (12)
Kind of huts on the hill (5)
Laura (5)
Laura lived there: ___ Tracey (5)
Laura's father (9)
London's country (7)
Mire (7)
Mrs. Stapleton (5)
Nature's night light (4)
Reason for behavior (6)
Receive from a will (7)

Relatives (3)
SH examined Mortimer's ___ stick (7)
SH saw the spy on this street (6)
Servant to Charles and Henry (9)
Sir Arthur Conan ___ (5)
Sir Charles had a bad one (5)
Sir Charles smoked one (5)
Sound of the hound (4)
Spaniel or hound, for example (3)
Stapleton fell ___ the mire. (4)
Stapleton's house (8)
The hound left this 20 feet from Charles (9)
The man on the ___ (3)
The spy rode in one. (3)
The whole of one's possessions (6)
To be introduced to someone (4)
Tried to kill Henry (9)
Walkway where Charles died (8)
Watson heard Mrs. B. doing this. (3)
Watson sent one to Holmes often (6)
___ Holmes (8)
___ on the Tor (3)

Hound of the Baskervilles Word Search 1 Answer Key

Words are placed backwards, forward, diagonally, up and down. Clues listed below can help you find the words. Circle the hidden vocabulary words in the maze.

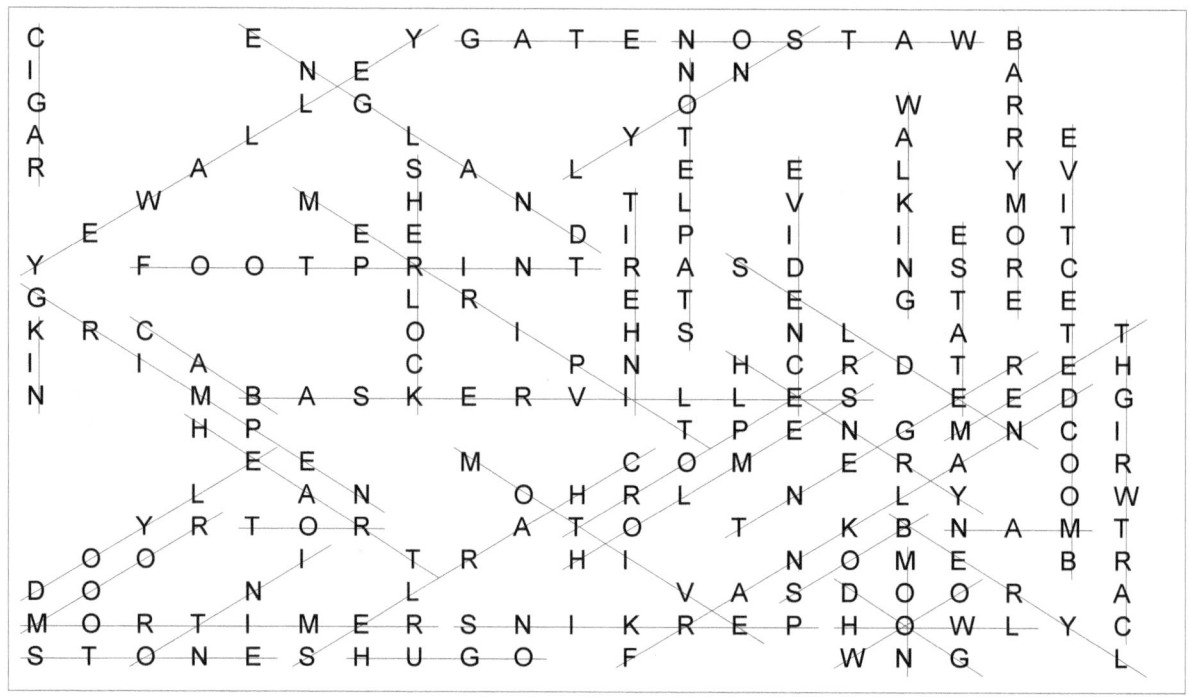

Bad luck place for the Baskervilles (4)
CB waited to meet LL there (4)
Charles's heir (5)
Chief detective on the Baskerville case (6)
Clues; Sherlock gathers this (8)
Convict (6)
Court towards marriage (3)
Died of heart failure (7)
Doctor to Charles (8)
Groom (7)
He sold out to the powers of evil (4)
Holmes or Watson, for example (9)
Holmes's assistant (6)
Holmes's boy helper (10)
Hound of the ___ (12)
Kind of huts on the hill (5)
Laura (5)
Laura lived there: ___ Tracey (5)
Laura's father (9)
London's country (7)
Mire (7)
Mrs. Stapleton (5)
Nature's night light (4)
Reason for behavior (6)
Receive from a will (7)

Relatives (3)
SH examined Mortimer's ___ stick (7)
SH saw the spy on this street (6)
Servant to Charles and Henry (9)
Sir Arthur Conan ___ (5)
Sir Charles had a bad one (5)
Sir Charles smoked one (5)
Sound of the hound (4)
Spaniel or hound, for example (3)
Stapleton fell ___ the mire. (4)
Stapleton's house (8)
The hound left this 20 feet from Charles (9)
The man on the ___ (3)
The spy rode in one. (3)
The whole of one's possessions (6)
To be introduced to someone (4)
Tried to kill Henry (9)
Walkway where Charles died (8)
Watson heard Mrs. B. doing this. (3)
Watson sent one to Holmes often (6)
___ Holmes (8)
___ on the Tor (3)

30
Copyrighted

Hound of the Baskervilles Word Search 2

Words are placed backwards, forward, diagonally, up and down. Clues listed below can help you find the words. Circle the hidden vocabulary words in the maze.

S	V	E	H	G	E	P	E	N	G	L	A	N	D	B	F	F	H	C	B	D
E	T	R	M	E	C	M	E	V	M	J	C	Q	R	Q	O	Z	G	H	Y	E
L	R	O	Q	S	N	V	O	R	Y	Q	M	A	W	N	O	G	L	A	S	T
L	W	M	N	R	E	R	S	R	K	H	G	D	Z	Z	T	L	M	R	B	E
I	Y	Y	Z	E	D	Y	Y	K	T	I	Q	N	B	H	P	E	M	L	V	C
V	S	R	D	X	I	E	G	H	C	I	N	D	L	F	R	B	F	E	F	T
R	G	R	D	G	V	W	I	G	T	P	M	S	T	R	I	Y	T	S	T	I
E	X	A	Y	V	E	A	T	N	B	S	N	E	I	T	N	W	F	D	S	V
K	K	B	D	V	X	L	B	I	H	W	D	P	R	D	T	H	M	L	E	E
S	P	N	I	C	S	L	F	K	Z	E	I	P	N	J	W	M	Y	Y	L	Z
A	R	T	Y	H	L	E	W	L	N	T	R	F	O	K	F	O	L	O	D	B
B	O	L	Y	K	F	Y	L	A	F	T	O	I	S	E	I	O	I	N	E	D
M	M	E	Q	C	A	R	T	W	R	I	G	H	T	L	G	N	R	S	N	H
H	T	S	W	O	G	C	X	O	Y	C	U	E	A	Y	T	N	R	A	O	Q
F	W	T	B	L	J	R	P	S	W	N	H	A	W	O	F	E	L	G	C	B
H	D	A	E	R	C	E	I	E	O	W	B	R	M	D	G	K	C	B	L	T
K	K	T	H	E	R	A	W	M	O	O	R	T	A	E	N	G	M	Y	R	R
P	A	E	O	H	C	Y	B	L	P	X	E	W	N	A	O	O	R	O	T	F
G	M	M	W	S	X	J	M	O	W	E	Q	T	R	D	O	E	T	R	V	V
T	G	V	L	F	G	J	B	H	M	H	N	F	W	C	B	C	W	Z	X	H

Bad luck place for the Baskervilles (4)
CB waited to meet LL there (4)
Charles's heir (5)
Chief detective on the Baskerville case (6)
Clues; Sherlock gathers this (8)
Convict (6)
Court towards marriage (3)
Died of heart failure (7)
Doctor to Charles (8)
Groom (7)
He sold out to the powers of evil (4)
Holmes or Watson, for example (9)
Holmes's assistant (6)
Holmes's boy helper (10)
Hound of the ___ (12)
Kind of huts on the hill (5)
Laura (5)
Laura lived there: ___ Tracey (5)
Laura's father (9)
London's country (7)
Mire (7)
Mrs. Stapleton (5)
Nature's night light (4)
Reason for behavior (6)
Receive from a will (7)

Relatives (3)
SH examined Mortimer's ___ stick (7)
SH saw the spy on this street (6)
Servant to Charles and Henry (9)
Sir Arthur Conan ___ (5)
Sir Charles had a bad one (5)
Sir Charles smoked one (5)
Sound of the hound (4)
Spaniel or hound, for example (3)
Stapleton fell ___ the mire. (4)
Stapleton's house (8)
The hound left this 20 feet from Charles (9)
The man on the ___ (3)
The spy rode in one. (3)
The whole of one's possessions (6)
To be introduced to someone (4)
Walkway where Charles died (8)
Watson heard Mrs. B. doing this. (3)
Watson sent one to Holmes often (6)
___ Holmes (8)
___ on the Tor (3)

Hound of the Baskervilles Word Search 2 Answer Key

Words are placed backwards, forward, diagonally, up and down. Clues listed below can help you find the words. Circle the hidden vocabulary words in the maze.

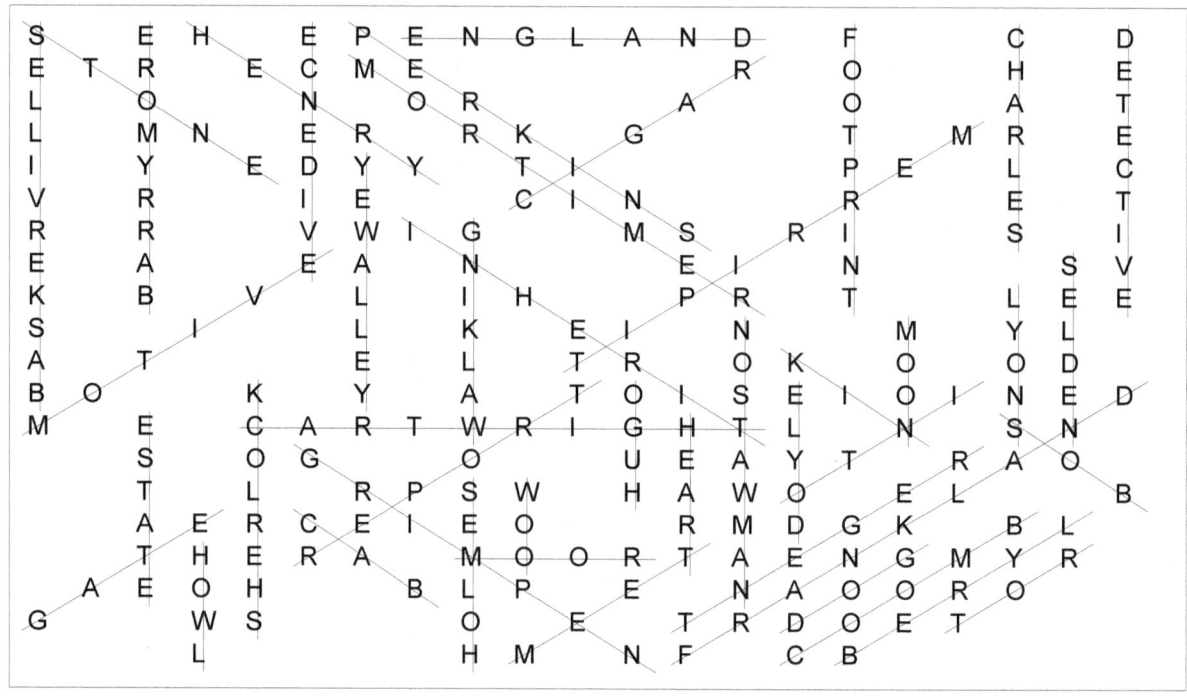

Bad luck place for the Baskervilles (4)
CB waited to meet LL there (4)
Charles's heir (5)
Chief detective on the Baskerville case (6)
Clues; Sherlock gathers this (8)
Convict (6)
Court towards marriage (3)
Died of heart failure (7)
Doctor to Charles (8)
Groom (7)
He sold out to the powers of evil (4)
Holmes or Watson, for example (9)
Holmes's assistant (6)
Holmes's boy helper (10)
Hound of the ___ (12)
Kind of huts on the hill (5)
Laura (5)
Laura lived there: ___ Tracey (5)
Laura's father (9)
London's country (7)
Mire (7)
Mrs. Stapleton (5)
Nature's night light (4)
Reason for behavior (6)
Receive from a will (7)

Relatives (3)
SH examined Mortimer's ___ stick (7)
SH saw the spy on this street (6)
Servant to Charles and Henry (9)
Sir Arthur Conan ___ (5)
Sir Charles had a bad one (5)
Sir Charles smoked one (5)
Sound of the hound (4)
Spaniel or hound, for example (3)
Stapleton fell ___ the mire. (4)
Stapleton's house (8)
The hound left this 20 feet from Charles (9)
The man on the ___ (3)
The spy rode in one. (3)
The whole of one's possessions (6)
To be introduced to someone (4)
Walkway where Charles died (8)
Watson heard Mrs. B. doing this. (3)
Watson sent one to Holmes often (6)
___ Holmes (8)
___ on the Tor (3)

Hound of the Baskervilles Word Search 3

Words are placed backwards, forward, diagonally, up and down. Words listed below are included in the maze. Circle the hidden vocabulary words in the maze.

```
M O T I V E V I D E N C E P Q H Y Z S T K
W E Y D N A L K N A R F M Z X V L Q N S V
D B R Z Z B A S K E R V I L L E S I T D G
F P E R K I N S M T H G I R W T R A C Y Z
P T P P I Z L I K M N K R V R P P D P F Z
S P B C M P T X E J C V Q W T L T R V F P
Y V C R L R I V G L H R W O E J Z C Q S Q
B C E K O H I T Q C A M O T S N B B Y R N
L Y S M Y T Z Z L C R F O C H L A E D A J
F P T G C N N R W T L N B C E R W Z O G K
C L A E M R N X O Q E O N M R A Z L T I B
G H T R O P E R L N S N O Y L M O O N C F
W E E V R N P G Y W J Q M L O Z B A I W K
D A T Z O G M W E D Q O E P C P M E P O D
V R D T R N I H E N R Y O C K H N S R O G
G T S O E I R T L E T G A V O G O O V Y D
S R Y D G K G Q Y X U B K Q L O O L L H L
K Q L L P L V R O H D Z C A M M M W M H Y
C E T A G A X F D S G K N N G M O B T E W
S M E E T W A T S O N D G I N H E R I T S
```

BARRYMORE	ESTATE	INTO	REPORT
BASKERVILLES	EVIDENCE	KIN	SELDEN
BERYL	FOOTPRINT	LYONS	SHERLOCK
CAB	FRANKLAND	MAN	SOB
CARTWRIGHT	GATE	MEET	STAPLETON
CHARLES	GRIMPEN	MERRIPIT	STONE
CIGAR	HEART	MOON	TOR
COOMB	HENRY	MOOR	WALKING
DETECTIVE	HOLMES	MORTIMER	WATSON
DOG	HOWL	MOTIVE	WOO
DOYLE	HUGO	PERKINS	YEWALLEY
ENGLAND	INHERIT	REGENT	

Hound of the Baskervilles Word Search 3 Answer Key

Words are placed backwards, forward, diagonally, up and down. Words listed below are included in the maze. Circle the hidden vocabulary words in the maze.

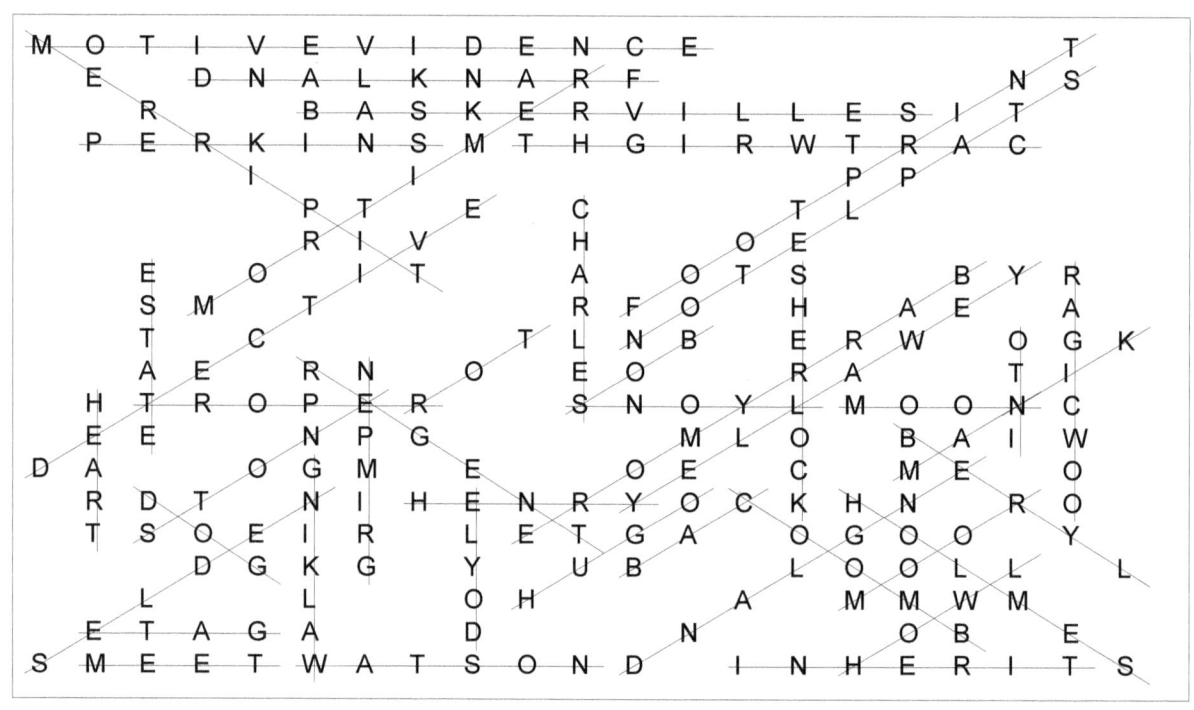

BARRYMORE	ESTATE	INTO	REPORT
BASKERVILLES	EVIDENCE	KIN	SELDEN
BERYL	FOOTPRINT	LYONS	SHERLOCK
CAB	FRANKLAND	MAN	SOB
CARTWRIGHT	GATE	MEET	STAPLETON
CHARLES	GRIMPEN	MERRIPIT	STONE
CIGAR	HEART	MOON	TOR
COOMB	HENRY	MOOR	WALKING
DETECTIVE	HOLMES	MORTIMER	WATSON
DOG	HOWL	MOTIVE	WOO
DOYLE	HUGO	PERKINS	YEWALLEY
ENGLAND	INHERIT	REGENT	

Hound of the Baskervilles Word Search 4

Words are placed backwards, forward, diagonally, up and down. Words listed below are included in the maze. Circle the hidden vocabulary words in the maze.

```
W S T A P L E T O N B A R R Y M O R E S F
A A Z M R W Y Q B A X A E E O A C Q S E G
L G T G B O Z O C B G Y M T P N H J T L W
K H T S S H C B N I C P I Z K O A V A D V
I I N T O H T C C S C V T B L H R O T E Y
N W D H B N U H N L E K R A H E L T E N X
G B M O O C G G D Z C I O S S A E L D G V
Y E W A L L E Y O F A N M K B R S R E L C
G G T T L Y M O G R R Q E E R T O T K A F
D N R L W R W E T A T P E R R O A K G N H
L E S I Q E E T S N W D T V M G T K D D R
M P T K M B C V J K R N T I M X N T H C V
D O X E F P N Z P L I G C L R S E T E Y Z
P Z O J C X E M H A G F Z L Y D G G L G E
Y E T N H T D N H N H R D E W Y E Y Y N L
M E R R I P I T Z D T J R S H E R L O C K
R X G K G W V V P R H L K V Q N S T D W L
R W C F I C E T E B Y D H R E Q S D M D Z
T I R E H N I M L R R C N H L Z F D Z F F
S G W B B Z S F O O T P R I N T R J D T S
```

BARRYMORE	ESTATE	INTO	REPORT
BASKERVILLES	EVIDENCE	KIN	SELDEN
BERYL	FOOTPRINT	LYONS	SHERLOCK
CAB	FRANKLAND	MAN	SOB
CARTWRIGHT	GATE	MEET	STAPLETON
CHARLES	GRIMPEN	MERRIPIT	STONE
CIGAR	HEART	MOON	TOR
COOMB	HENRY	MOOR	WALKING
DETECTIVE	HOLMES	MORTIMER	WATSON
DOG	HOWL	MOTIVE	WOO
DOYLE	HUGO	PERKINS	YEWALLEY
ENGLAND	INHERIT	REGENT	

Hound of the Baskervilles Word Search 4 Answer Key

Words are placed backwards, forward, diagonally, up and down. Words listed below are included in the maze. Circle the hidden vocabulary words in the maze.

BARRYMORE	ESTATE	INTO	REPORT
BASKERVILLES	EVIDENCE	KIN	SELDEN
BERYL	FOOTPRINT	LYONS	SHERLOCK
CAB	FRANKLAND	MAN	SOB
CARTWRIGHT	GATE	MEET	STAPLETON
CHARLES	GRIMPEN	MERRIPIT	STONE
CIGAR	HEART	MOON	TOR
COOMB	HENRY	MOOR	WALKING
DETECTIVE	HOLMES	MORTIMER	WATSON
DOG	HOWL	MOTIVE	WOO
DOYLE	HUGO	PERKINS	YEWALLEY
ENGLAND	INHERIT	REGENT	

Hound of the Baskervilles Crossword 1

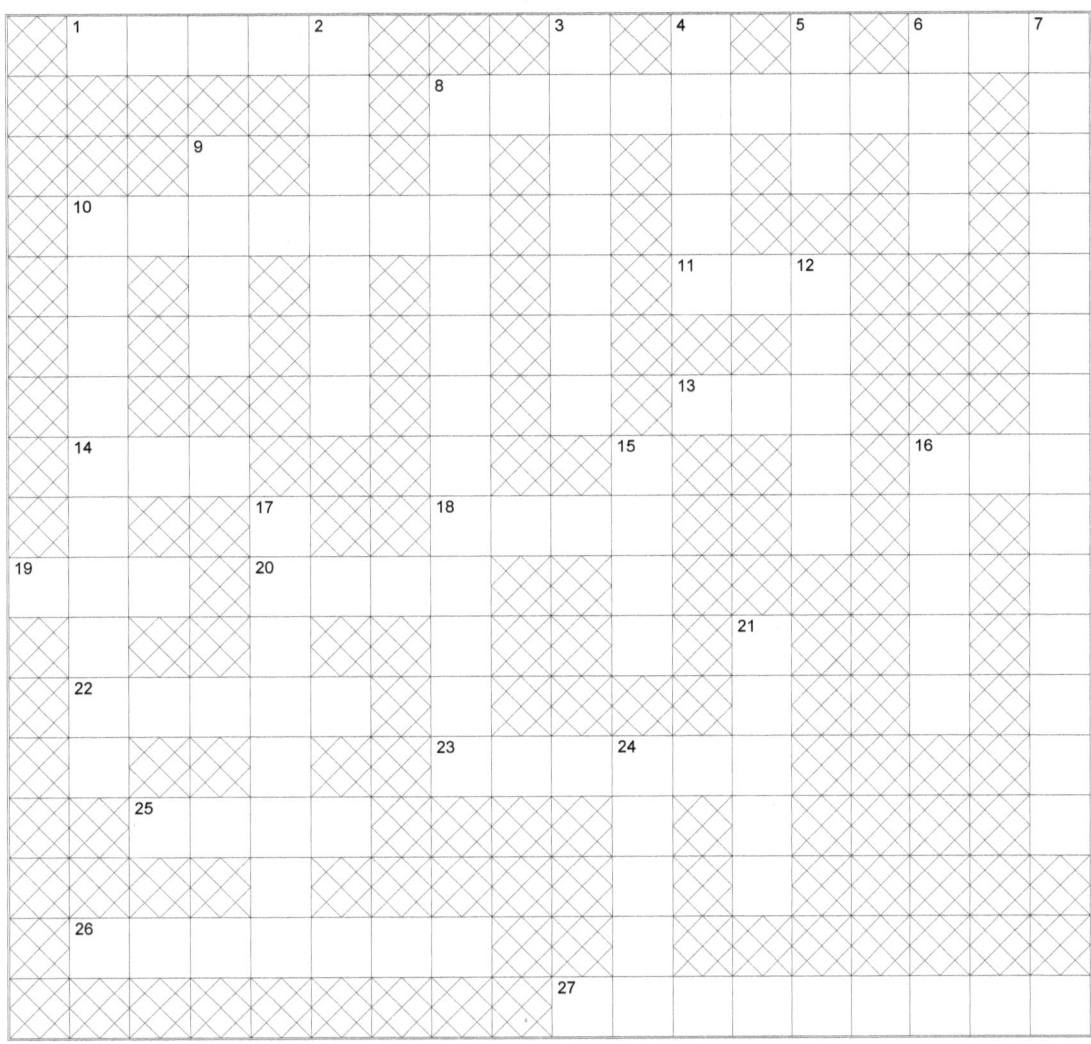

Across
1. Kind of huts on the hill
6. ___ on the Tor
8. Servant to Charles and Henry
10. Died of heart failure
11. Watson heard Mrs. B. doing this.
13. The man on the ___
14. Court towards marriage
16. The spy rode in one.
18. Stapleton fell ___ the mire.
19. Relatives
20. Sound of the hound
22. Sir Charles had a bad one
23. Convict
25. Nature's night light
26. Groom
27. Holmes or Watson, for example

Down
2. London's country
3. Mire
4. Laura
5. Spaniel or hound, for example
6. To be introduced to someone
7. Hotel
8. Hound of the ___
9. CB waited to meet LL there
10. Holmes's boy helper
12. Mrs. Stapleton
15. Bad luck place for the Baskervilles
16. Laura lived there: ___ Tracey
17. ___ Holmes
21. Charles's heir
24. Sir Arthur Conan ___

Hound of the Baskervilles Crossword 1 Answer Key

	1 S	T	O	2 N	E			3 G		4 L		5 D		6 M	A	7 N
				N		8 B	A	R	R	Y	M	O	R	E		O
			9 G		G	A		I		O		G		E		R
		10 C	H	A	R	L	E	S		M		N		T		T
		A		T		A		K		P		11 S	12 O	B		H
		R		E		N		E		E		E				U
		T			D		R		N		13 T	O	R			M
		14 W	O	O						15 M				16 C	A	B
		R		17 S		18 I	N	T	O			L		O		E
19 K	I	N		H	O	W	L							O		R
		G		E		L			R		21 H			M		L
		22 H	E	A	R	T					E			B		A
		T		L		23 S	E	L	24 D	E	N					N
			25 M	O	O	N			O		R					D
				C					Y		Y					
		26 P	E	R	K	I	N	S			L					
								27 D	E	T	E	C	T	I	V	E

Across
1. Kind of huts on the hill
6. ___ on the Tor
8. Servant to Charles and Henry
10. Died of heart failure
11. Watson heard Mrs. B. doing this.
13. The man on the ___
14. Court towards marriage
16. The spy rode in one.
18. Stapleton fell ___ the mire.
19. Relatives
20. Sound of the hound
22. Sir Charles had a bad one
23. Convict
25. Nature's night light
26. Groom
27. Holmes or Watson, for example

Down
2. London's country
3. Mire
4. Laura
5. Spaniel or hound, for example
6. To be introduced to someone
7. Hotel
8. Hound of the ___
9. CB waited to meet LL there
10. Holmes's boy helper
12. Mrs. Stapleton
15. Bad luck place for the Baskervilles
16. Laura lived there: ___ Tracey
17. ___ Holmes
21. Charles's heir
24. Sir Arthur Conan ___

38
Copyrighted

Hound of the Baskervilles Crossword 2

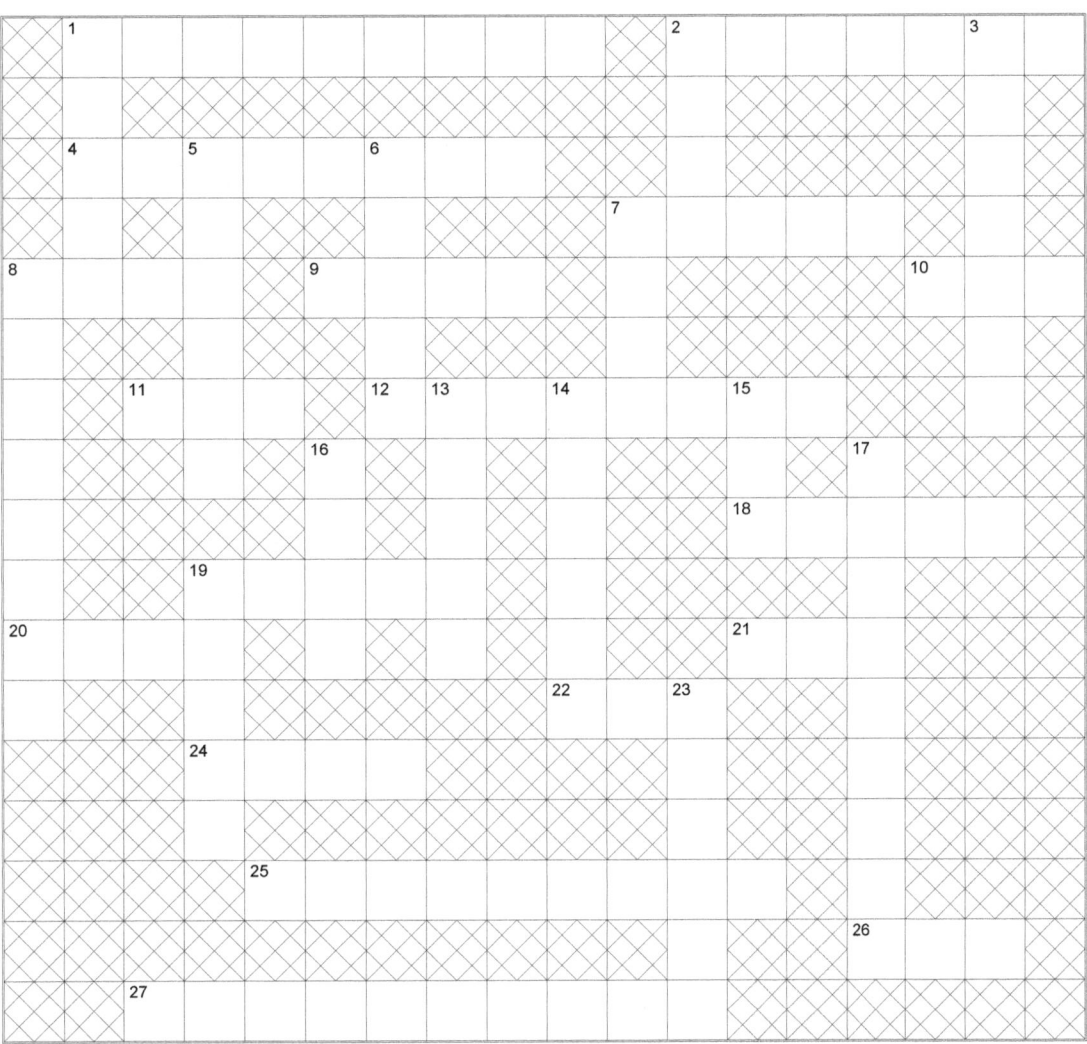

Across
1. Holmes or Watson, for example
2. Mire
4. Walkway where Charles died
7. Charles's heir
8. To be introduced to someone
9. Nature's night light
10. ___ on the Tor
11. Watson heard Mrs. B. doing this.
12. ___ Holmes
18. Mrs. Stapleton
19. Sir Charles smoked one
20. Stapleton fell ___ the mire.
21. Relatives
22. The man on the ___
24. Bad luck place for the Baskervilles
25. Tried to kill Henry
26. Spaniel or hound, for example
27. Holmes's boy helper

Down
1. Sir Arthur Conan ___
2. CB waited to meet LL there
3. London's country
5. Holmes's assistant
6. Laura
7. Sound of the hound
8. Stapleton's house
13. Sir Charles had a bad one
14. SH saw the spy on this street
15. The spy rode in one.
16. He sold out to the powers of evil
17. Laura's father
19. Laura lived there: ___ Tracey
23. Watson sent one to Holmes often

Hound of the Baskervilles Crossword 2 Answer Key

	1 D	E	T	E	C	T	I	V	E		2 G	R	I	M	P	3 E	N
	O										A					N	
	4 Y	E	5 W	A	L	6 L	E	Y			T					G	
	L		A			Y			7 H	E	N	R	Y			L	
8 M	E	E	T		9 M	O	O	N		O				10 M	A	N	
E			S			N				W						N	
R		11 S	O	B		12 S	H	13 E	R	14 L	O	15 C	K			D	
R		N		16 H		E		E		E		A		17 F			
I				U		A		G				18 B	E	R	Y	L	
P		19 C	I	G	A	R		E						A			
20 I	N	T	O		O		T		N		21 K	I	N				
T		O					22 T	O	23 R				K				
		24 M	O	O	R				E				L				
		B							P				A				
		25 S	T	A	P	L	E	T	O	N			N				
									R			26 D	O	G			
		27 C	A	R	T	W	R	I	G	H	T						

Across
1. Holmes or Watson, for example
2. Mire
4. Walkway where Charles died
7. Charles's heir
8. To be introduced to someone
9. Nature's night light
10. ___ on the Tor
11. Watson heard Mrs. B. doing this.
12. ___ Holmes
18. Mrs. Stapleton
19. Sir Charles smoked one
20. Stapleton fell ___ the mire.
21. Relatives
22. The man on the ___
24. Bad luck place for the Baskervilles
25. Tried to kill Henry
26. Spaniel or hound, for example
27. Holmes's boy helper

Down
1. Sir Arthur Conan ___
2. CB waited to meet LL there
3. London's country
5. Holmes's assistant
6. Laura
7. Sound of the hound
8. Stapleton's house
13. Sir Charles had a bad one
14. SH saw the spy on this street
15. The spy rode in one.
16. He sold out to the powers of evil
17. Laura's father
19. Laura lived there: ___ Tracey
23. Watson sent one to Holmes often

Hound of the Baskervilles Crossword 3

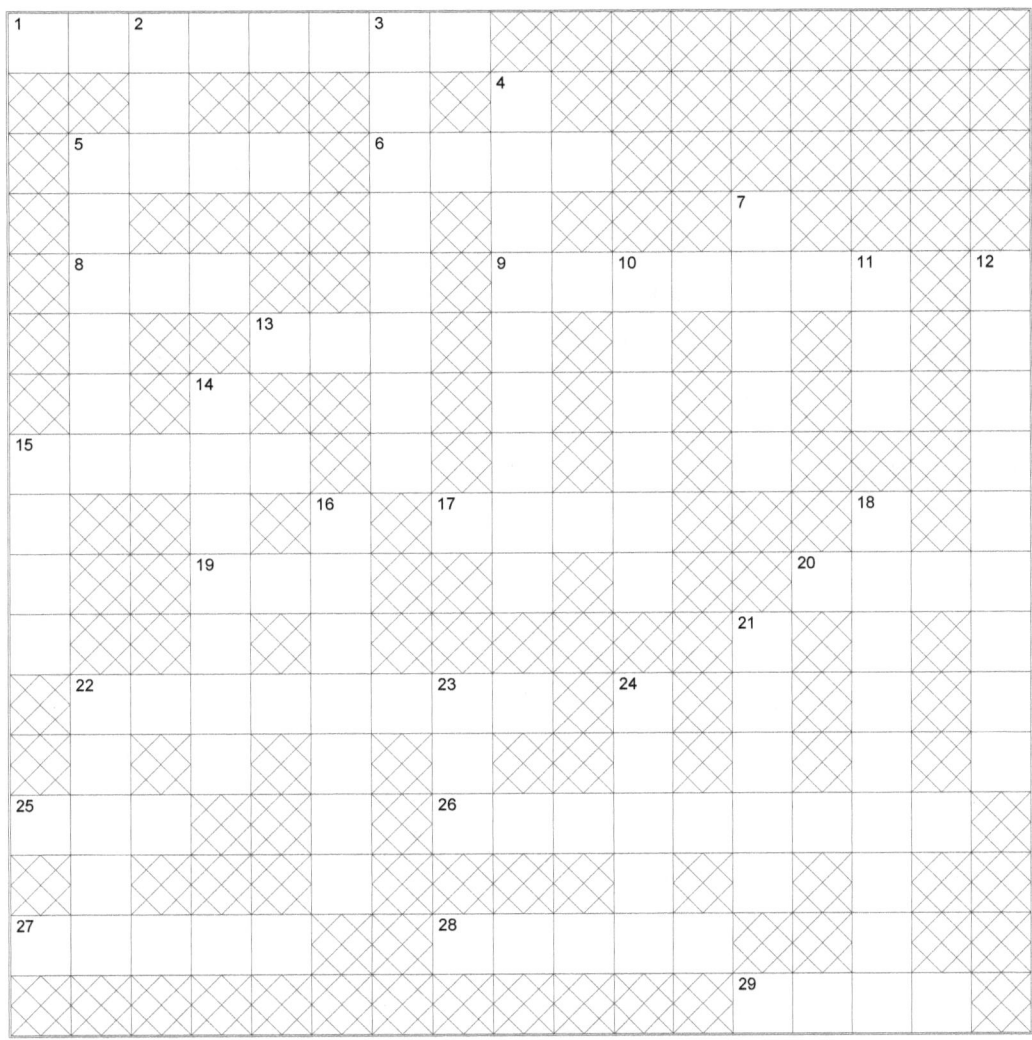

Across
1. Walkway where Charles died
5. Bad luck place for the Baskervilles
6. Stapleton fell ___ the mire.
8. The man on the ___
9. Groom
13. Relatives
15. Charles's heir
17. Nature's night light
19. ___ on the Tor
20. Sound of the hound
22. ___ Holmes
25. Spaniel or hound, for example
26. Servant to Charles and Henry
27. Sir Charles had a bad one
28. Sir Arthur Conan ___
29. CB waited to meet LL there

Down
2. Court towards marriage
3. Clues; Sherlock gathers this
4. Tried to kill Henry
5. Reason for behavior
7. Sir Charles smoked one
10. SH saw the spy on this street
11. Watson heard Mrs. B. doing this.
12. Laura's father
14. Mire
15. He sold out to the powers of evil
16. London's country
18. The hound left this 20 feet from Charles
21. Laura lived there: ___ Tracey
22. Kind of huts on the hill
23. The spy rode in one.
24. Mrs. Stapleton

Hound of the Baskervilles Crossword 3 Answer Key

	1 Y	2 E	W	A	L	L	3 E	Y					
		O					V		4 S				
	5 M	O	O	R		6 I	N	T	O				
		O				D			A		7 C		
	8 T	O	R			E		9 P	10 E	R	K	11 I	N	S	12 F
		I		13 K	I	N		L		E		G		O		R
		V		14 G				C		E		A		B		A
15 H	E	N	R	Y				E		T		E				N
U				I		16 E		17 M	O	O	N			18 F		K
G				19 M	A	N				N		T		20 H	O	W	L
O						P		G				21 C		O		A
		22 S	H	E	R	L	O	C	K		24 B		O		T		N
		T			N			A			A		E		O		P		D
25 D	O	G				N		26 B	A	R	R	Y	M	O	R	E
		N				D				Y		B			I	
27 H	E	A	R	T			28 D	O	Y	L	E			N	
										29 G	A	T	E	

Across
1. Walkway where Charles died
5. Bad luck place for the Baskervilles
6. Stapleton fell ___ the mire.
8. The man on the ___
9. Groom
13. Relatives
15. Charles's heir
17. Nature's night light
19. ___ on the Tor
20. Sound of the hound
22. ___ Holmes
25. Spaniel or hound, for example
26. Servant to Charles and Henry
27. Sir Charles had a bad one
28. Sir Arthur Conan ___
29. CB waited to meet LL there

Down
2. Court towards marriage
3. Clues; Sherlock gathers this
4. Tried to kill Henry
5. Reason for behavior
7. Sir Charles smoked one
10. SH saw the spy on this street
11. Watson heard Mrs. B. doing this.
12. Laura's father
14. Mire
15. He sold out to the powers of evil
16. London's country
18. The hound left this 20 feet from Charles
21. Laura lived there: ___ Tracey
22. Kind of huts on the hill
23. The spy rode in one.
24. Mrs. Stapleton

Hound of the Baskervilles Crossword 4

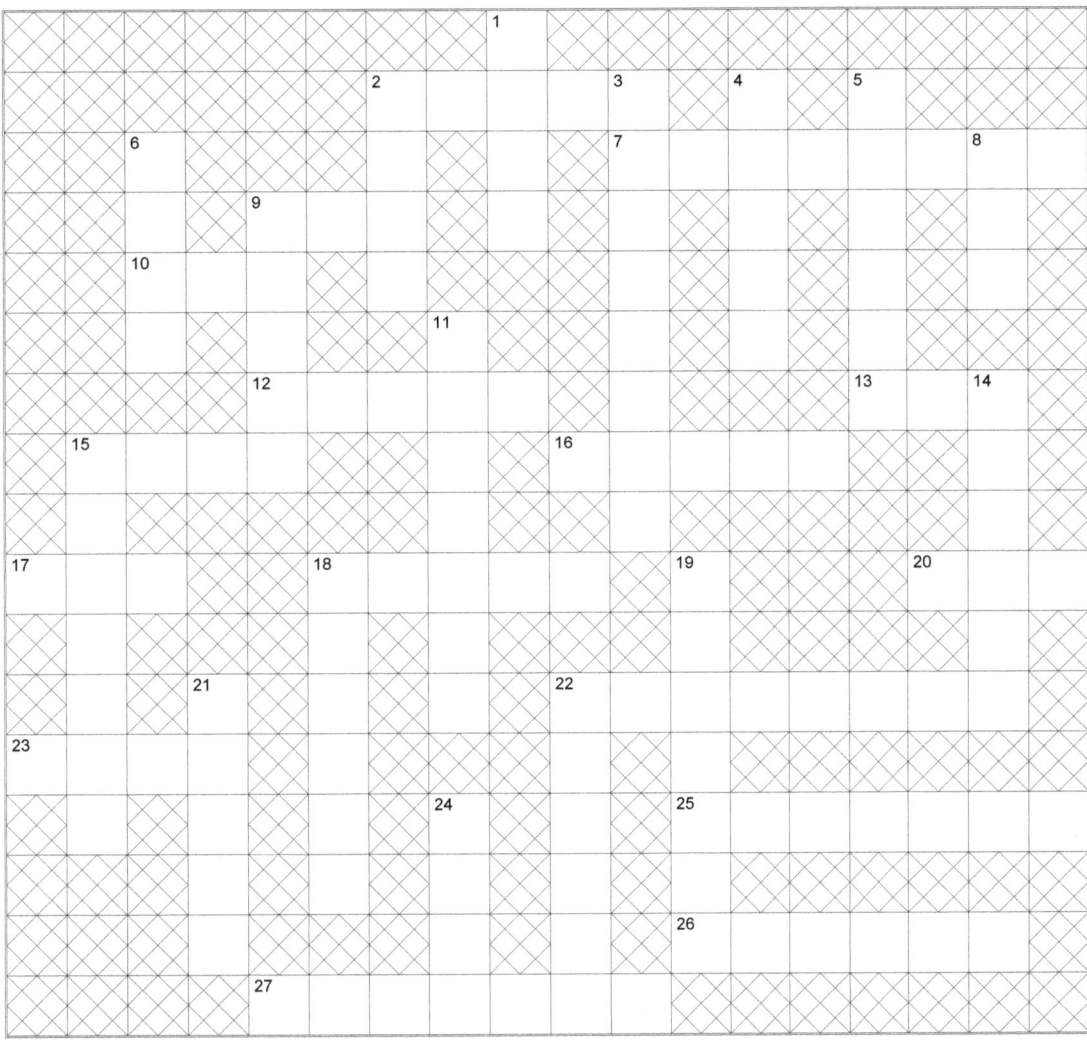

Across
2. Charles's heir
7. Clues; Sherlock gathers this
9. Spaniel or hound, for example
10. Court towards marriage
12. Laura
13. The man on the ___
15. CB waited to meet LL there
16. Mrs. Stapleton
17. Relatives
18. Sir Charles had a bad one
20. Watson heard Mrs. B. doing this.
22. Stapleton's house
23. To be introduced to someone
25. Receive from a will
26. Convict
27. Died of heart failure

Down
1. Stapleton fell ___ the mire.
2. He sold out to the powers of evil
3. Walkway where Charles died
4. Sir Charles smoked one
5. SH saw the spy on this street
6. Sound of the hound
8. The spy rode in one.
9. Sir Arthur Conan ___
11. London's country
14. Watson sent one to Holmes often
15. Mire
18. Chief detective on the Baskerville case
19. Groom
21. Kind of huts on the hill
22. Reason for behavior
24. Bad luck place for the Baskervilles

Hound of the Baskervilles Crossword 4 Answer Key

Across
2. Charles's heir
7. Clues; Sherlock gathers this
9. Spaniel or hound, for example
10. Court towards marriage
12. Laura
13. The man on the ___
15. CB waited to meet LL there
16. Mrs. Stapleton
17. Relatives
18. Sir Charles had a bad one
20. Watson heard Mrs. B. doing this.
22. Stapleton's house
23. To be introduced to someone
25. Receive from a will
26. Convict
27. Died of heart failure

Down
1. Stapleton fell ___ the mire.
2. He sold out to the powers of evil
3. Walkway where Charles died
4. Sir Charles smoked one
5. SH saw the spy on this street
6. Sound of the hound
8. The spy rode in one.
9. Sir Arthur Conan ___
11. London's country
14. Watson sent one to Holmes often
15. Mire
18. Chief detective on the Baskerville case
19. Groom
21. Kind of huts on the hill
22. Reason for behavior
24. Bad luck place for the Baskervilles

Hound of the Baskervilles

PERKINS	STAPLETON	HOWL	BERYL	DOG
WATSON	CARTWRIGHT	BARRYMORE	INTO	FOOTPRINT
NORTHUMBERLAND	YEWALLEY	FREE SPACE	KIN	GATE
MORTIMER	CIGAR	HOLMES	MAN	REGENT
SHERLOCK	EVIDENCE	MOON	SOB	STONE

Hound of the Baskervilles

HENRY	DETECTIVE	SELDEN	FRANKLAND	CAB
MOOR	INHERIT	COOMB	WOO	REPORT
MEET	GRIMPEN	FREE SPACE	HUGO	DOYLE
ESTATE	TOR	HEART	CHARLES	LYONS
MERRIPIT	BASKERVILLES	WALKING	STONE	SOB

Hound of the Baskervilles

WATSON	STONE	KIN	ENGLAND	LYONS
PERKINS	SOB	FRANKLAND	HUGO	HENRY
WOO	MOTIVE	FREE SPACE	WALKING	INTO
YEWALLEY	DETECTIVE	REGENT	HEART	NORTHUMBERLAND
EVIDENCE	HOLMES	CARTWRIGHT	BARRYMORE	MOOR

Hound of the Baskervilles

MORTIMER	CAB	MOON	GATE	TOR
INHERIT	HOWL	FOOTPRINT	CHARLES	CIGAR
BASKERVILLES	REPORT	FREE SPACE	MERRIPIT	DOG
GRIMPEN	ESTATE	COOMB	MAN	MEET
BERYL	SELDEN	STAPLETON	MOOR	BARRYMORE

Hound of the Baskervilles

DOYLE	PERKINS	GRIMPEN	YEWALLEY	STONE
WALKING	INHERIT	CARTWRIGHT	HEART	SHERLOCK
CIGAR	HOLMES	FREE SPACE	MORTIMER	WOO
COOMB	DETECTIVE	MAN	DOG	HUGO
LYONS	GATE	BERYL	TOR	CAB

Hound of the Baskervilles

EVIDENCE	REPORT	CHARLES	INTO	REGENT
KIN	BARRYMORE	FOOTPRINT	WATSON	FRANKLAND
HOWL	NORTHUMBERLAND	FREE SPACE	MOTIVE	SELDEN
MOOR	BASKERVILLES	ESTATE	ENGLAND	HENRY
MEET	MOON	STAPLETON	CAB	TOR

Hound of the Baskervilles

GATE	MORTIMER	TOR	FOOTPRINT	REGENT
MOTIVE	YEWALLEY	MEET	SELDEN	BASKERVILLES
HUGO	CARTWRIGHT	FREE SPACE	LYONS	INTO
EVIDENCE	HEART	COOMB	MOOR	MAN
BARRYMORE	DETECTIVE	DOYLE	CAB	HOWL

Hound of the Baskervilles

GRIMPEN	DOG	STONE	PERKINS	MERRIPIT
WALKING	ESTATE	KIN	HOLMES	HENRY
CIGAR	FRANKLAND	FREE SPACE	SOB	INHERIT
ENGLAND	CHARLES	SHERLOCK	WOO	BERYL
STAPLETON	MOON	REPORT	HOWL	CAB

Hound of the Baskervilles

SHERLOCK	MOTIVE	INHERIT	CIGAR	INTO
COOMB	DOG	CAB	SELDEN	REPORT
TOR	REGENT	FREE SPACE	MERRIPIT	ENGLAND
CARTWRIGHT	GRIMPEN	YEWALLEY	MORTIMER	BARRYMORE
DOYLE	SOB	LYONS	HUGO	NORTHUMBERLAND

Hound of the Baskervilles

BERYL	WALKING	STONE	FOOTPRINT	HOWL
MAN	KIN	PERKINS	MOON	HENRY
EVIDENCE	WOO	FREE SPACE	HOLMES	GATE
CHARLES	BASKERVILLES	WATSON	HEART	MEET
DETECTIVE	MOOR	STAPLETON	NORTHUMBERLAND	HUGO

Hound of the Baskervilles

CHARLES	MOOR	WALKING	GRIMPEN	NORTHUMBERLAND
INHERIT	HENRY	TOR	MOON	HEART
REPORT	STAPLETON	FREE SPACE	MAN	SOB
DETECTIVE	SHERLOCK	BASKERVILLES	ENGLAND	MEET
EVIDENCE	COOMB	KIN	WATSON	CARTWRIGHT

Hound of the Baskervilles

WOO	MORTIMER	HOWL	DOG	ESTATE
HOLMES	MERRIPIT	GATE	YEWALLEY	STONE
REGENT	BARRYMORE	FREE SPACE	LYONS	CIGAR
CAB	MOTIVE	FRANKLAND	DOYLE	BERYL
SELDEN	FOOTPRINT	HUGO	CARTWRIGHT	WATSON

Hound of the Baskervilles

HOWL	HENRY	MOOR	MORTIMER	MAN
FOOTPRINT	TOR	MOON	ENGLAND	SHERLOCK
REGENT	DOG	FREE SPACE	BARRYMORE	WATSON
COOMB	PERKINS	YEWALLEY	SOB	CARTWRIGHT
STAPLETON	REPORT	LYONS	GATE	INHERIT

Hound of the Baskervilles

DOYLE	KIN	FRANKLAND	HUGO	HOLMES
GRIMPEN	NORTHUMBERLAND	MOTIVE	EVIDENCE	INTO
CIGAR	ESTATE	FREE SPACE	SELDEN	BERYL
MERRIPIT	MEET	WOO	WALKING	HEART
DETECTIVE	CAB	CHARLES	INHERIT	GATE

Hound of the Baskervilles

ENGLAND	KIN	BARRYMORE	FOOTPRINT	BASKERVILLES
CARTWRIGHT	INHERIT	TOR	PERKINS	WALKING
HUGO	HENRY	FREE SPACE	SELDEN	DETECTIVE
EVIDENCE	MEET	CIGAR	INTO	HOLMES
STONE	STAPLETON	REPORT	GRIMPEN	YEWALLEY

Hound of the Baskervilles

CAB	SHERLOCK	FRANKLAND	LYONS	REGENT
CHARLES	MAN	MOOR	ESTATE	GATE
MERRIPIT	DOYLE	FREE SPACE	MOTIVE	HOWL
BERYL	COOMB	SOB	MOON	DOG
HEART	MORTIMER	WOO	YEWALLEY	GRIMPEN

Hound of the Baskervilles

PERKINS	WATSON	NORTHUMBERLAND	MERRIPIT	SELDEN
HEART	BASKERVILLES	DETECTIVE	BARRYMORE	STONE
HOLMES	INHERIT	FREE SPACE	ESTATE	TOR
GATE	CHARLES	FRANKLAND	SHERLOCK	KIN
WOO	HUGO	DOG	REGENT	ENGLAND

Hound of the Baskervilles

MOOR	STAPLETON	GRIMPEN	INTO	REPORT
LYONS	FOOTPRINT	EVIDENCE	YEWALLEY	CARTWRIGHT
HOWL	WALKING	FREE SPACE	CAB	CIGAR
COOMB	MAN	MEET	BERYL	SOB
DOYLE	MORTIMER	MOTIVE	ENGLAND	REGENT

Hound of the Baskervilles

MOTIVE	KIN	CAB	WALKING	HENRY
HOLMES	NORTHUMBERLAND	MOOR	EVIDENCE	ENGLAND
FOOTPRINT	SELDEN	FREE SPACE	DOG	INHERIT
HEART	PERKINS	CARTWRIGHT	DETECTIVE	DOYLE
REGENT	GATE	ESTATE	WATSON	FRANKLAND

Hound of the Baskervilles

MOON	YEWALLEY	GRIMPEN	BERYL	BASKERVILLES
MORTIMER	MERRIPIT	MEET	WOO	HOWL
COOMB	STONE	FREE SPACE	MAN	HUGO
SHERLOCK	STAPLETON	REPORT	LYONS	SOB
BARRYMORE	INTO	CHARLES	FRANKLAND	WATSON

Hound of the Baskervilles

MOOR	WALKING	MAN	YEWALLEY	REPORT
CAB	FRANKLAND	WATSON	MEET	MERRIPIT
REGENT	STONE	FREE SPACE	INHERIT	BARRYMORE
WOO	MOTIVE	ENGLAND	MORTIMER	LYONS
STAPLETON	ESTATE	DOYLE	HOLMES	MOON

Hound of the Baskervilles

KIN	HUGO	HENRY	SHERLOCK	GATE
NORTHUMBERLAND	BASKERVILLES	INTO	DETECTIVE	BERYL
TOR	HOWL	FREE SPACE	DOG	CIGAR
COOMB	GRIMPEN	CARTWRIGHT	HEART	CHARLES
FOOTPRINT	SOB	SELDEN	MOON	HOLMES

Hound of the Baskervilles

REGENT	SOB	YEWALLEY	INTO	MAN
EVIDENCE	LYONS	HUGO	WATSON	HOWL
ESTATE	HOLMES	FREE SPACE	GRIMPEN	MERRIPIT
STAPLETON	TOR	MEET	FOOTPRINT	COOMB
CARTWRIGHT	BASKERVILLES	ENGLAND	MORTIMER	BARRYMORE

Hound of the Baskervilles

SELDEN	MOON	FRANKLAND	CIGAR	KIN
PERKINS	CHARLES	MOTIVE	STONE	WOO
HENRY	WALKING	FREE SPACE	MOOR	DETECTIVE
GATE	INHERIT	BERYL	DOYLE	NORTHUMBERLAND
SHERLOCK	HEART	CAB	BARRYMORE	MORTIMER

Hound of the Baskervilles

HOWL	DOG	STONE	MOON	ESTATE
BASKERVILLES	DOYLE	WOO	MOTIVE	FRANKLAND
HEART	FOOTPRINT	FREE SPACE	REGENT	MERRIPIT
STAPLETON	BARRYMORE	MORTIMER	MEET	TOR
ENGLAND	BERYL	NORTHUMBERLAND	CHARLES	CAB

Hound of the Baskervilles

GATE	INHERIT	MOOR	SOB	CIGAR
INTO	LYONS	GRIMPEN	PERKINS	SELDEN
REPORT	KIN	FREE SPACE	CARTWRIGHT	WALKING
DETECTIVE	HUGO	MAN	HOLMES	WATSON
HENRY	SHERLOCK	YEWALLEY	CAB	CHARLES

Hound of the Baskervilles

CIGAR	ESTATE	HOLMES	REPORT	DOG
NORTHUMBERLAND	INTO	HOWL	GRIMPEN	FRANKLAND
MAN	SELDEN	FREE SPACE	DETECTIVE	TOR
SOB	WATSON	PERKINS	INHERIT	REGENT
HEART	DOYLE	BARRYMORE	MERRIPIT	HUGO

Hound of the Baskervilles

MOTIVE	MEET	SHERLOCK	GATE	MOON
YEWALLEY	STAPLETON	KIN	CARTWRIGHT	MORTIMER
LYONS	COOMB	FREE SPACE	HENRY	STONE
EVIDENCE	WALKING	ENGLAND	CHARLES	FOOTPRINT
WOO	BERYL	CAB	HUGO	MERRIPIT

Hound of the Baskervilles

FOOTPRINT	BARRYMORE	DETECTIVE	GRIMPEN	COOMB
ESTATE	WATSON	HEART	HOLMES	HENRY
MERRIPIT	MORTIMER	FREE SPACE	HOWL	NORTHUMBERLAND
MOTIVE	SOB	DOG	FRANKLAND	ENGLAND
PERKINS	BASKERVILLES	REPORT	MOON	REGENT

Hound of the Baskervilles

MOOR	GATE	SELDEN	TOR	LYONS
WALKING	MAN	STONE	WOO	CHARLES
HUGO	SHERLOCK	FREE SPACE	BERYL	EVIDENCE
CIGAR	INHERIT	YEWALLEY	MEET	KIN
INTO	DOYLE	CARTWRIGHT	REGENT	MOON

Hound of the Baskervilles

CARTWRIGHT	INTO	GRIMPEN	ESTATE	COOMB
HOLMES	MOOR	SELDEN	GATE	DOYLE
BARRYMORE	INHERIT	FREE SPACE	HUGO	WALKING
REPORT	TOR	SOB	SHERLOCK	REGENT
BERYL	MOTIVE	MEET	DOG	CIGAR

Hound of the Baskervilles

MORTIMER	HOWL	NORTHUMBERLAND	FRANKLAND	WATSON
HENRY	FOOTPRINT	HEART	CHARLES	STONE
LYONS	PERKINS	FREE SPACE	CAB	YEWALLEY
MERRIPIT	DETECTIVE	ENGLAND	BASKERVILLES	WOO
MAN	STAPLETON	MOON	CIGAR	DOG

Hound of the Baskervilles Vocabulary Word List

No.	Word	Clue/Definition
1.	ABHOR	Loathe; hate
2.	AGAPE	In a state of amazement with the mouth wide open
3.	AMID	In the middle of
4.	AMPLE	Enough
5.	APPARITION	Ghostly figure
6.	APPROBATION	Official approval
7.	AUDACIOUS	Daring; bold
8.	AUSTERE	Stern; somber
9.	AVAILED	Helped; made use of
10.	BALUSTRADED	Having a rail supported by posts
11.	BOURGEOIS	Middle class
12.	BRUSQUELY	Abruptly
13.	CATASTROPHE	A great, often sudden disaster
14.	CIRCUMSPECT	Prudent; mindful of circumstances
15.	CLANDESTINE	Secret; done in secret
16.	COMMUTATION	Substitution; exchange
17.	CONNOISSEUR	A person of informed and discriminating taste
18.	CORROBORATED	Supported with other evidence
19.	DELUGE	A heavy downpour
20.	DISMAY	Upset; alarm; disillusion; loss of enthusiasm
21.	ENDEAVOR	Try
22.	EQUESTRIAN	Horse or relating to horses
23.	ERRONEOUS	Mistaken
24.	EXECUTOR	Person appointed to carry out a will
25.	FIEND	Spirit; demon
26.	FINESSE	Skillful, delicate handling
27.	FURTIVE	Stealthy; sneaky
28.	HEIR	One who inherits
29.	IMPLICIT	Unquestioning
30.	INCESSANT	Constant; continual
31.	INDELIBLY	Permanently
32.	INDUCE	Influence; persuade
33.	INERT	Unable to move
34.	INEXORABLY	Relentlessly
35.	INJUNCTIONS	Directives; orders
36.	LUMINOUS	Emitting light
37.	MALIGNANCY	Evil
38.	MELANCHOLY	Gloomy
39.	MULLIONED	With divided panes
40.	PRESUME	Assume; take for granted
41.	PUGNACIOUS	Belligerent; has a fighting nature
42.	SILHOUETTED	Looking dark against a light background
43.	SKEIN	Length of thread or yarn rolled into a loose ball
44.	SOLICITATIONS	Pleas; petitions
45.	SPECTRAL	Ghostly
46.	TENACITY	Perseverance
47.	UNMITIGATED	Without qualification or exception; absolute
48.	VEXATION	Annoyance
49.	VIGIL	Period of watchfulness or waiting
50.	VILE	Loathsome; disgusting; objectionable

Hound of the Baskervilles Vocabulary Fill In The Blanks 1

_____ 1. A person of informed and discriminating taste

_____ 2. Ghostly

_____ 3. Middle class

_____ 4. Annoyance

_____ 5. Period of watchfulness or waiting

_____ 6. Daring; bold

_____ 7. A heavy downpour

_____ 8. Stern; somber

_____ 9. Try

_____ 10. Loathe; hate

_____ 11. Emitting light

_____ 12. Ghostly figure

_____ 13. Secret; done in secret

_____ 14. Evil

_____ 15. Upset; alarm; disillusion; loss of enthusiasm

_____ 16. Substitution; exchange

_____ 17. In the middle of

_____ 18. Prudent; mindful of circumstances

_____ 19. Stealthy; sneaky

_____ 20. Abruptly

Hound of the Baskervilles Vocabulary Fill In The Blanks 1 Answer Key

CONNOISSEUR	1. A person of informed and discriminating taste
SPECTRAL	2. Ghostly
BOURGEOIS	3. Middle class
VEXATION	4. Annoyance
VIGIL	5. Period of watchfulness or waiting
AUDACIOUS	6. Daring; bold
DELUGE	7. A heavy downpour
AUSTERE	8. Stern; somber
ENDEAVOR	9. Try
ABHOR	10. Loathe; hate
LUMINOUS	11. Emitting light
APPARITION	12. Ghostly figure
CLANDESTINE	13. Secret; done in secret
MALIGNANCY	14. Evil
DISMAY	15. Upset; alarm; disillusion; loss of enthusiasm
COMMUTATION	16. Substitution; exchange
AMID	17. In the middle of
CIRCUMSPECT	18. Prudent; mindful of circumstances
FURTIVE	19. Stealthy; sneaky
BRUSQUELY	20. Abruptly

Hound of the Baskervilles Vocabulary Fill In The Blanks 2

_____ 1. A heavy downpour
_____ 2. Perseverance
_____ 3. Constant; continual
_____ 4. Spirit; demon
_____ 5. Enough
_____ 6. Directives; orders
_____ 7. In the middle of
_____ 8. Stealthy; sneaky
_____ 9. Daring; bold
_____ 10. Horse or relating to horses
_____ 11. Mistaken
_____ 12. Influence; persuade
_____ 13. Period of watchfulness or waiting
_____ 14. Relentlessly
_____ 15. Pleas; petitions
_____ 16. Person appointed to carry out a will
_____ 17. Unable to move
_____ 18. Unquestioning
_____ 19. Skillful, delicate handling
_____ 20. One who inherits

Hound of the Baskervilles Vocabulary Fill In The Blanks 2 Answer Key

DELUGE	1.	A heavy downpour
TENACITY	2.	Perseverance
INCESSANT	3.	Constant; continual
FIEND	4.	Spirit; demon
AMPLE	5.	Enough
INJUNCTIONS	6.	Directives; orders
AMID	7.	In the middle of
FURTIVE	8.	Stealthy; sneaky
AUDACIOUS	9.	Daring; bold
EQUESTRIAN	10.	Horse or relating to horses
ERRONEOUS	11.	Mistaken
INDUCE	12.	Influence; persuade
VIGIL	13.	Period of watchfulness or waiting
INEXORABLY	14.	Relentlessly
SOLICITATIONS	15.	Pleas; petitions
EXECUTOR	16.	Person appointed to carry out a will
INERT	17.	Unable to move
IMPLICIT	18.	Unquestioning
FINESSE	19.	Skillful, delicate handling
HEIR	20.	One who inherits

Hound of the Baskervilles Vocabulary Fill In The Blanks 3

_____ 1. With divided panes
_____ 2. Annoyance
_____ 3. Supported with other evidence
_____ 4. Stern; somber
_____ 5. Emitting light
_____ 6. Without qualification or exception; absolute
_____ 7. Constant; continual
_____ 8. Period of watchfulness or waiting
_____ 9. Influence; persuade
_____ 10. Enough
_____ 11. Skillful, delicate handling
_____ 12. Relentlessly
_____ 13. Permanently
_____ 14. One who inherits
_____ 15. Evil
_____ 16. Secret; done in secret
_____ 17. Ghostly
_____ 18. Looking dark against a light background
_____ 19. Prudent; mindful of circumstances
_____ 20. Spirit; demon

Hound of the Baskervilles Vocabulary Fill In The Blanks 3 Answer Key

MULLIONED	1.	With divided panes
VEXATION	2.	Annoyance
CORROBORATED	3.	Supported with other evidence
AUSTERE	4.	Stern; somber
LUMINOUS	5.	Emitting light
UNMITIGATED	6.	Without qualification or exception; absolute
INCESSANT	7.	Constant; continual
VIGIL	8.	Period of watchfulness or waiting
INDUCE	9.	Influence; persuade
AMPLE	10.	Enough
FINESSE	11.	Skillful, delicate handling
INEXORABLY	12.	Relentlessly
INDELIBLY	13.	Permanently
HEIR	14.	One who inherits
MALIGNANCY	15.	Evil
CLANDESTINE	16.	Secret; done in secret
SPECTRAL	17.	Ghostly
SILHOUETTED	18.	Looking dark against a light background
CIRCUMSPECT	19.	Prudent; mindful of circumstances
FIEND	20.	Spirit; demon

Hound of the Baskervilles Vocabulary Fill In The Blanks 4

_____ 1. Enough

_____ 2. Having a rail supported by posts

_____ 3. In the middle of

_____ 4. Helped; made use of

_____ 5. Upset; alarm; disillusion; loss of enthusiasm

_____ 6. One who inherits

_____ 7. Try

_____ 8. Secret; done in secret

_____ 9. Constant; continual

_____ 10. Daring; bold

_____ 11. Ghostly figure

_____ 12. Person appointed to carry out a will

_____ 13. Loathe; hate

_____ 14. Unquestioning

_____ 15. Skillful, delicate handling

_____ 16. Without qualification or exception; absolute

_____ 17. Gloomy

_____ 18. Perseverance

_____ 19. Directives; orders

_____ 20. Abruptly

Hound of the Baskervilles Vocabulary Fill In The Blanks 4 Answer Key

AMPLE	1. Enough
BALUSTRADED	2. Having a rail supported by posts
AMID	3. In the middle of
AVAILED	4. Helped; made use of
DISMAY	5. Upset; alarm; disillusion; loss of enthusiasm
HEIR	6. One who inherits
ENDEAVOR	7. Try
CLANDESTINE	8. Secret; done in secret
INCESSANT	9. Constant; continual
AUDACIOUS	10. Daring; bold
APPARITION	11. Ghostly figure
EXECUTOR	12. Person appointed to carry out a will
ABHOR	13. Loathe; hate
IMPLICIT	14. Unquestioning
FINESSE	15. Skillful, delicate handling
UNMITIGATED	16. Without qualification or exception; absolute
MELANCHOLY	17. Gloomy
TENACITY	18. Perseverance
INJUNCTIONS	19. Directives; orders
BRUSQUELY	20. Abruptly

Hound of the Baskervilles Vocabulary Matching 1

___ 1. HEIR   A. Enough
___ 2. APPARITION   B. Pleas; petitions
___ 3. INERT   C. Substitution; exchange
___ 4. VEXATION   D. Relentlessly
___ 5. APPROBATION   E. Belligerent; has a fighting nature
___ 6. CLANDESTINE   F. Unable to move
___ 7. AMID   G. In the middle of
___ 8. AVAILED   H. Evil
___ 9. CONNOISSEUR   I. Influence; persuade
___ 10. MALIGNANCY   J. Unquestioning
___ 11. IMPLICIT   K. Horse or relating to horses
___ 12. EQUESTRIAN   L. Perseverance
___ 13. PRESUME   M. One who inherits
___ 14. COMMUTATION   N. Ghostly
___ 15. SPECTRAL   O. Secret; done in secret
___ 16. SKEIN   P. Official approval
___ 17. AMPLE   Q. Length of thread or yarn rolled into a loose ball
___ 18. FINESSE   R. Skillful, delicate handling
___ 19. SOLICITATIONS   S. Loathe; hate
___ 20. AUDACIOUS   T. Assume; take for granted
___ 21. INDUCE   U. A person of informed and discriminating taste
___ 22. TENACITY   V. Ghostly figure
___ 23. ABHOR   W. Annoyance
___ 24. INEXORABLY   X. Helped; made use of
___ 25. PUGNACIOUS   Y. Daring; bold

Hound of the Baskervilles Vocabulary Matching 1 Answer Key

M - 1. HEIR
V - 2. APPARITION
F - 3. INERT
W - 4. VEXATION
P - 5. APPROBATION
O - 6. CLANDESTINE
G - 7. AMID
X - 8. AVAILED
U - 9. CONNOISSEUR
H - 10. MALIGNANCY
J - 11. IMPLICIT
K - 12. EQUESTRIAN
T - 13. PRESUME
C - 14. COMMUTATION
N - 15. SPECTRAL
Q - 16. SKEIN
A - 17. AMPLE
R - 18. FINESSE
B - 19. SOLICITATIONS
Y - 20. AUDACIOUS
I - 21. INDUCE
L - 22. TENACITY
S - 23. ABHOR
D - 24. INEXORABLY
E - 25. PUGNACIOUS

A. Enough
B. Pleas; petitions
C. Substitution; exchange
D. Relentlessly
E. Belligerent; has a fighting nature
F. Unable to move
G. In the middle of
H. Evil
I. Influence; persuade
J. Unquestioning
K. Horse or relating to horses
L. Perseverance
M. One who inherits
N. Ghostly
O. Secret; done in secret
P. Official approval
Q. Length of thread or yarn rolled into a loose ball
R. Skillful, delicate handling
S. Loathe; hate
T. Assume; take for granted
U. A person of informed and discriminating taste
V. Ghostly figure
W. Annoyance
X. Helped; made use of
Y. Daring; bold

Hound of the Baskervilles Vocabulary Matching 2

___ 1. CATASTROPHE A. Loathe; hate
___ 2. INJUNCTIONS B. Having a rail supported by posts
___ 3. CORROBORATED C. Middle class
___ 4. SILHOUETTED D. Official approval
___ 5. EQUESTRIAN E. Skillful, delicate handling
___ 6. APPROBATION F. Directives; orders
___ 7. LUMINOUS G. One who inherits
___ 8. CONNOISSEUR H. Abruptly
___ 9. FINESSE I. Perseverance
___ 10. FIEND J. Period of watchfulness or waiting
___ 11. HEIR K. Emitting light
___ 12. ENDEAVOR L. With divided panes
___ 13. ABHOR M. In a state of amazement with the mouth wide open
___ 14. CIRCUMSPECT N. Looking dark against a light background
___ 15. TENACITY O. Horse or relating to horses
___ 16. UNMITIGATED P. Helped; made use of
___ 17. SOLICITATIONS Q. Spirit; demon
___ 18. BRUSQUELY R. Mistaken
___ 19. ERRONEOUS S. Prudent; mindful of circumstances
___ 20. AVAILED T. Supported with other evidence
___ 21. BOURGEOIS U. Without qualification or exception; absolute
___ 22. MULLIONED V. Try
___ 23. BALUSTRADED W. Pleas; petitions
___ 24. VIGIL X. A person of informed and discriminating taste
___ 25. AGAPE Y. A great, often sudden disaster

Hound of the Baskervilles Vocabulary Matching 2 Answer Key

Y - 1.	CATASTROPHE	A.	Loathe; hate
F - 2.	INJUNCTIONS	B.	Having a rail supported by posts
T - 3.	CORROBORATED	C.	Middle class
N - 4.	SILHOUETTED	D.	Official approval
O - 5.	EQUESTRIAN	E.	Skillful, delicate handling
D - 6.	APPROBATION	F.	Directives; orders
K - 7.	LUMINOUS	G.	One who inherits
X - 8.	CONNOISSEUR	H.	Abruptly
E - 9.	FINESSE	I.	Perseverance
Q -10.	FIEND	J.	Period of watchfulness or waiting
G -11.	HEIR	K.	Emitting light
V -12.	ENDEAVOR	L.	With divided panes
A -13.	ABHOR	M.	In a state of amazement with the mouth wide open
S -14.	CIRCUMSPECT	N.	Looking dark against a light background
I - 15.	TENACITY	O.	Horse or relating to horses
U -16.	UNMITIGATED	P.	Helped; made use of
W -17.	SOLICITATIONS	Q.	Spirit; demon
H -18.	BRUSQUELY	R.	Mistaken
R -19.	ERRONEOUS	S.	Prudent; mindful of circumstances
P -20.	AVAILED	T.	Supported with other evidence
C -21.	BOURGEOIS	U.	Without qualification or exception; absolute
L -22.	MULLIONED	V.	Try
B -23.	BALUSTRADED	W.	Pleas; petitions
J -24.	VIGIL	X.	A person of informed and discriminating taste
M -25.	AGAPE	Y.	A great, often sudden disaster

Hound of the Baskervilles Vocabulary Matching 3

___ 1. CIRCUMSPECT   A. In the middle of
___ 2. INCESSANT   B. In a state of amazement with the mouth wide open
___ 3. EQUESTRIAN   C. One who inherits
___ 4. INEXORABLY   D. Upset; alarm; disillusion; loss of enthusiasm
___ 5. CONNOISSEUR   E. Looking dark against a light background
___ 6. SOLICITATIONS   F. Relentlessly
___ 7. CLANDESTINE   G. Secret; done in secret
___ 8. COMMUTATION   H. Enough
___ 9. CATASTROPHE   I. Daring; bold
___10. VIGIL   J. Pleas; petitions
___11. AMID   K. Prudent; mindful of circumstances
___12. HEIR   L. Evil
___13. DISMAY   M. Constant; continual
___14. CORROBORATED   N. Without qualification or exception; absolute
___15. AUDACIOUS   O. Horse or relating to horses
___16. AGAPE   P. A great, often sudden disaster
___17. INDELIBLY   Q. Spirit; demon
___18. UNMITIGATED   R. With divided panes
___19. SILHOUETTED   S. Emitting light
___20. AMPLE   T. Person appointed to carry out a will
___21. FIEND   U. A person of informed and discriminating taste
___22. EXECUTOR   V. Substitution; exchange
___23. MALIGNANCY   W. Permanently
___24. MULLIONED   X. Period of watchfulness or waiting
___25. LUMINOUS   Y. Supported with other evidence

Hound of the Baskervilles Vocabulary Matching 3 Answer Key

K - 1. CIRCUMSPECT		A. In the middle of
M - 2. INCESSANT		B. In a state of amazement with the mouth wide open
O - 3. EQUESTRIAN		C. One who inherits
F - 4. INEXORABLY		D. Upset; alarm; disillusion; loss of enthusiasm
U - 5. CONNOISSEUR		E. Looking dark against a light background
J - 6. SOLICITATIONS		F. Relentlessly
G - 7. CLANDESTINE		G. Secret; done in secret
V - 8. COMMUTATION		H. Enough
P - 9. CATASTROPHE		I. Daring; bold
X - 10. VIGIL		J. Pleas; petitions
A - 11. AMID		K. Prudent; mindful of circumstances
C - 12. HEIR		L. Evil
D - 13. DISMAY		M. Constant; continual
Y - 14. CORROBORATED		N. Without qualification or exception; absolute
I - 15. AUDACIOUS		O. Horse or relating to horses
B - 16. AGAPE		P. A great, often sudden disaster
W - 17. INDELIBLY		Q. Spirit; demon
N - 18. UNMITIGATED		R. With divided panes
E - 19. SILHOUETTED		S. Emitting light
H - 20. AMPLE		T. Person appointed to carry out a will
Q - 21. FIEND		U. A person of informed and discriminating taste
T - 22. EXECUTOR		V. Substitution; exchange
L - 23. MALIGNANCY		W. Permanently
R - 24. MULLIONED		X. Period of watchfulness or waiting
S - 25. LUMINOUS		Y. Supported with other evidence

Hound of the Baskervilles Vocabulary Matching 4

___ 1. PUGNACIOUS   A. Ghostly
___ 2. INEXORABLY   B. Helped; made use of
___ 3. FINESSE   C. Secret; done in secret
___ 4. INERT   D. Annoyance
___ 5. APPROBATION   E. Prudent; mindful of circumstances
___ 6. AGAPE   F. Stern; somber
___ 7. BALUSTRADED   G. Official approval
___ 8. APPARITION   H. Loathsome; disgusting; objectionable
___ 9. SPECTRAL   I. Without qualification or exception; absolute
___10. AUSTERE   J. Upset; alarm; disillusion; loss of enthusiasm
___11. CLANDESTINE   K. Having a rail supported by posts
___12. VEXATION   L. In a state of amazement with the mouth wide open
___13. EQUESTRIAN   M. Skillful, delicate handling
___14. VILE   N. Perseverance
___15. AVAILED   O. Substitution; exchange
___16. AUDACIOUS   P. Constant; continual
___17. HEIR   Q. Relentlessly
___18. CIRCUMSPECT   R. One who inherits
___19. LUMINOUS   S. Belligerent; has a fighting nature
___20. UNMITIGATED   T. Daring; bold
___21. COMMUTATION   U. Emitting light
___22. DISMAY   V. Directives; orders
___23. INJUNCTIONS   W. Horse or relating to horses
___24. TENACITY   X. Ghostly figure
___25. INCESSANT   Y. Unable to move

Hound of the Baskervilles Vocabulary Matching 4 Answer Key

S - 1. PUGNACIOUS   A. Ghostly
Q - 2. INEXORABLY   B. Helped; made use of
M - 3. FINESSE   C. Secret; done in secret
Y - 4. INERT   D. Annoyance
G - 5. APPROBATION   E. Prudent; mindful of circumstances
L - 6. AGAPE   F. Stern; somber
K - 7. BALUSTRADED   G. Official approval
X - 8. APPARITION   H. Loathsome; disgusting; objectionable
A - 9. SPECTRAL   I. Without qualification or exception; absolute
F - 10. AUSTERE   J. Upset; alarm; disillusion; loss of enthusiasm
C - 11. CLANDESTINE   K. Having a rail supported by posts
D - 12. VEXATION   L. In a state of amazement with the mouth wide open
W - 13. EQUESTRIAN   M. Skillful, delicate handling
H - 14. VILE   N. Perseverance
B - 15. AVAILED   O. Substitution; exchange
T - 16. AUDACIOUS   P. Constant; continual
R - 17. HEIR   Q. Relentlessly
E - 18. CIRCUMSPECT   R. One who inherits
U - 19. LUMINOUS   S. Belligerent; has a fighting nature
I - 20. UNMITIGATED   T. Daring; bold
O - 21. COMMUTATION   U. Emitting light
J - 22. DISMAY   V. Directives; orders
V - 23. INJUNCTIONS   W. Horse or relating to horses
N - 24. TENACITY   X. Ghostly figure
P - 25. INCESSANT   Y. Unable to move

Hound of the Baskervilles Vocabulary Magic Squares 1

Match the definition with the vocabulary word. Put your answers in the magic squares below. When your answers are correct, all columns and rows will add to the same number.

A. VIGIL
B. ABHOR
C. LUMINOUS
D. VEXATION
E. INDUCE
F. AUDACIOUS
G. DELUGE
H. AVAILED
I. APPROBATION
J. SPECTRAL
K. CONNOISSEUR
L. CORROBORATED
M. AGAPE
N. EQUESTRIAN
O. ENDEAVOR
P. VILE

1. Emitting light
2. Ghostly
3. Daring; bold
4. Try
5. Loathsome; disgusting; objectionable
6. Influence; persuade
7. Official approval
8. Annoyance
9. In a state of amazement with the mouth wide open
10. Helped; made use of
11. Supported with other evidence
12. Period of watchfulness or waiting
13. Loathe; hate
14. A person of informed and discriminating taste
15. A heavy downpour
16. Horse or relating to horses

A= 12	B= 13	C= 1	D= 8
E= 6	F= 3	G= 15	H= 10
I= 7	J= 2	K= 14	L= 11
M= 9	N= 16	O= 4	P= 5

Hound of the Baskervilles Vocabulary Magic Squares 1 Answer Key

Match the definition with the vocabulary word. Put your answers in the magic squares below. When your answers are correct, all columns and rows will add to the same number.

A. VIGIL
B. ABHOR
C. LUMINOUS
D. VEXATION
E. INDUCE
F. AUDACIOUS
G. DELUGE
H. AVAILED
I. APPROBATION
J. SPECTRAL
K. CONNOISSEUR
L. CORROBORATED
M. AGAPE
N. EQUESTRIAN
O. ENDEAVOR
P. VILE

1. Emitting light
2. Ghostly
3. Daring; bold
4. Try
5. Loathsome; disgusting; objectionable
6. Influence; persuade
7. Official approval
8. Annoyance
9. In a state of amazement with the mouth wide open
10. Helped; made use of
11. Supported with other evidence
12. Period of watchfulness or waiting
13. Loathe; hate
14. A person of informed and discriminating taste
15. A heavy downpour
16. Horse or relating to horses

A=12	B=13	C=1	D=8
E=6	F=3	G=15	H=10
I=7	J=2	K=14	L=11
M=9	N=16	O=4	P=5

Hound of the Baskervilles Vocabulary Magic Squares 2

Match the definition with the vocabulary word. Put your answers in the magic squares below. When your answers are correct, all columns and rows will add to the same number.

A. EXECUTOR
B. SPECTRAL
C. INDUCE
D. PRESUME
E. CORROBORATED
F. VEXATION
G. FURTIVE
H. AUSTERE
I. INERT
J. MALIGNANCY
K. TENACITY
L. DISMAY
M. CONNOISSEUR
N. SOLICITATIONS
O. MELANCHOLY
P. INDELIBLY

1. Stern; somber
2. Person appointed to carry out a will
3. Ghostly
4. Stealthy; sneaky
5. Evil
6. Gloomy
7. Permanently
8. Unable to move
9. Perseverance
10. Pleas; petitions
11. A person of informed and discriminating taste
12. Upset; alarm; disillusion; loss of enthusiasm
13. Supported with other evidence
14. Assume; take for granted
15. Influence; persuade
16. Annoyance

A=	B=	C=	D=
E=	F=	G=	H=
I=	J=	K=	L=
M=	N=	O=	P=

Hound of the Baskervilles Vocabulary Magic Squares 2 Answer Key

Match the definition with the vocabulary word. Put your answers in the magic squares below. When your answers are correct, all columns and rows will add to the same number.

A. EXECUTOR
B. SPECTRAL
C. INDUCE
D. PRESUME
E. CORROBORATED
F. VEXATION
G. FURTIVE
H. AUSTERE
I. INERT
J. MALIGNANCY
K. TENACITY
L. DISMAY
M. CONNOISSEUR
N. SOLICITATIONS
O. MELANCHOLY
P. INDELIBLY

1. Stern; somber
2. Person appointed to carry out a will
3. Ghostly
4. Stealthy; sneaky
5. Evil
6. Gloomy
7. Permanently
8. Unable to move
9. Perseverance
10. Pleas; petitions
11. A person of informed and discriminating taste
12. Upset; alarm; disillusion; loss of enthusiasm
13. Supported with other evidence
14. Assume; take for granted
15. Influence; persuade
16. Annoyance

A=2	B=3	C=15	D=14
E=13	F=16	G=4	H=1
I=8	J=5	K=9	L=12
M=11	N=10	O=6	P=7

Hound of the Baskervilles Vocabulary Magic Squares 3

Match the definition with the vocabulary word. Put your answers in the magic squares below. When your answers are correct, all columns and rows will add to the same number.

A. ABHOR
B. APPARITION
C. VILE
D. VEXATION
E. FIEND
F. INCESSANT
G. FINESSE
H. BALUSTRADED
I. INDELIBLY
J. VIGIL
K. AUSTERE
L. AUDACIOUS
M. BOURGEOIS
N. AMPLE
O. CLANDESTINE
P. COMMUTATION

1. Having a rail supported by posts
2. Middle class
3. Ghostly figure
4. Stern; somber
5. Period of watchfulness or waiting
6. Loathsome; disgusting; objectionable
7. Substitution; exchange
8. Spirit; demon
9. Secret; done in secret
10. Constant; continual
11. Permanently
12. Annoyance
13. Loathe; hate
14. Daring; bold
15. Skillful, delicate handling
16. Enough

A=	B=	C=	D=
E=	F=	G=	H=
I=	J=	K=	L=
M=	N=	O=	P=

Hound of the Baskervilles Vocabulary Magic Squares 3 Answer Key

Match the definition with the vocabulary word. Put your answers in the magic squares below. When your answers are correct, all columns and rows will add to the same number.

A. ABHOR
B. APPARITION
C. VILE
D. VEXATION
E. FIEND
F. INCESSANT
G. FINESSE
H. BALUSTRADED
I. INDELIBLY
J. VIGIL
K. AUSTERE
L. AUDACIOUS
M. BOURGEOIS
N. AMPLE
O. CLANDESTINE
P. COMMUTATION

1. Having a rail supported by posts
2. Middle class
3. Ghostly figure
4. Stern; somber
5. Period of watchfulness or waiting
6. Loathsome; disgusting; objectionable
7. Substitution; exchange
8. Spirit; demon
9. Secret; done in secret
10. Constant; continual
11. Permanently
12. Annoyance
13. Loathe; hate
14. Daring; bold
15. Skillful, delicate handling
16. Enough

A=13	B=3	C=6	D=12
E=8	F=10	G=15	H=1
I=11	J=5	K=4	L=14
M=2	N=16	O=9	P=7

Hound of the Baskervilles Vocabulary Magic Squares 4

Match the definition with the vocabulary word. Put your answers in the magic squares below. When your answers are correct, all columns and rows will add to the same number.

A. SPECTRAL
B. AGAPE
C. CONNOISSEUR
D. SKEIN
E. SILHOUETTED
F. HEIR
G. INCESSANT
H. MELANCHOLY
I. BALUSTRADED
J. TENACITY
K. AMID
L. EQUESTRIAN
M. APPARITION
N. AUSTERE
O. DELUGE
P. DISMAY

1. Gloomy
2. Ghostly figure
3. In a state of amazement with the mouth wide open
4. In the middle of
5. Perseverance
6. A person of informed and discriminating taste
7. Upset; alarm; disillusion; loss of enthusiasm
8. Looking dark against a light background
9. A heavy downpour
10. One who inherits
11. Having a rail supported by posts
12. Length of thread or yarn rolled into a loose ball
13. Ghostly
14. Horse or relating to horses
15. Constant; continual
16. Stern; somber

A=	B=	C=	D=
E=	F=	G=	H=
I=	J=	K=	L=
M=	N=	O=	P=

Hound of the Baskervilles Vocabulary Magic Squares 4 Answer Key

Match the definition with the vocabulary word. Put your answers in the magic squares below. When your answers are correct, all columns and rows will add to the same number.

A. SPECTRAL
B. AGAPE
C. CONNOISSEUR
D. SKEIN
E. SILHOUETTED
F. HEIR
G. INCESSANT
H. MELANCHOLY
I. BALUSTRADED
J. TENACITY
K. AMID
L. EQUESTRIAN
M. APPARITION
N. AUSTERE
O. DELUGE
P. DISMAY

1. Gloomy
2. Ghostly figure
3. In a state of amazement with the mouth wide open
4. In the middle of
5. Perseverance
6. A person of informed and discriminating taste
7. Upset; alarm; disillusion; loss of enthusiasm
8. Looking dark against a light background
9. A heavy downpour
10. One who inherits
11. Having a rail supported by posts
12. Length of thread or yarn rolled into a loose ball
13. Ghostly
14. Horse or relating to horses
15. Constant; continual
16. Stern; somber

A=13	B=3	C=6	D=12
E=8	F=10	G=15	H=1
I=11	J=5	K=4	L=14
M=2	N=16	O=9	P=7

Hound of the Baskervilles Vocabulary Word Search 1

Words are placed backwards, forward, diagonally, up and down. Clues listed below can help you find the words. Circle the hidden vocabulary words in the maze.

```
I M P L I C I T L F R O V A E D N E V X M
N C S P L A L B K Y L B A R O X E N I D E
D V E X A T I O N V D E R J L S S K G C L
E W V R Q A C H S K M O N S T F N M I S A
L X W C L S Q J G U N C Y R L F O L L I N
I P Z M N T W L S E N R D D U R I P Y L C
B V H I Z R W E O Y O K S R D C T D D H H
L H E V R O R U M T F X T S H I C Z I O O
Y K T C E P S M U C R I C S U O N I M U L
S H F P I H T C L N V V N D H A U E A E Y
B W A C N E E D L E M B V E I Y J Y R T A
N G P O C X N E I F P I R R S F N G Z T U
A T Y N E L A L O J L P T U G S I T F E D
R Q B N S S C U N E X S X I S C E E B D A
I A O O S L I G E Q E Z H D G Q G S N S C
N R U I A N T E D U C R S E S A U L P D I
D Q R S N M Y P Q H O S Z L I N T E J L O
U S G S T L P E K H Q R G I W R C E L T U
C D E E S E W L B Z J B W A F T C P D Y S
E H O U T K R A E B Y X G V R B F V C V G
B G I R W M V E P P U G N A C I O U S B C
S W S D W Y C N A N G I L A M D I S M A Y
```

A great, often sudden disaster (11)
A heavy downpour (6)
A person of informed and discriminating taste (11)
Abruptly (9)
Annoyance (8)
Assume; take for granted (7)
Belligerent; has a fighting nature (10)
Constant; continual (9)
Daring; bold (9)
Directives; orders (11)
Emitting light (8)
Enough (5)
Evil (10)
Ghostly (8)
Gloomy (10)
Helped; made use of (7)
Horse or relating to horses (10)
In a state of amazement with the mouth wide open (5)
In the middle of (4)
Influence; persuade (6)
Length of thread or yarn rolled into a loose ball (5)
Loathe; hate (5)
Loathsome; disgusting; objectionable (4)
Looking dark against a light background (11)
Middle class (9)
Mistaken (9)
One who inherits (4)
Period of watchfulness or waiting (5)
Permanently (9)
Perseverance (8)
Person appointed to carry out a will (8)
Prudent; mindful of circumstances (11)
Relentlessly (10)
Skillful, delicate handling (7)
Spirit; demon (5)
Stealthy; sneaky (7)
Stern; somber (7)
Try (8)
Unable to move (5)
Unquestioning (8)
Upset; alarm; disillusion; loss of enthusiasm (6)
With divided panes (9)
Without qualification or exception; absolute (11)

Hound of the Baskervilles Vocabulary Word Search 1 Answer Key

Words are placed backwards, forward, diagonally, up and down. Clues listed below can help you find the words. Circle the hidden vocabulary words in the maze.

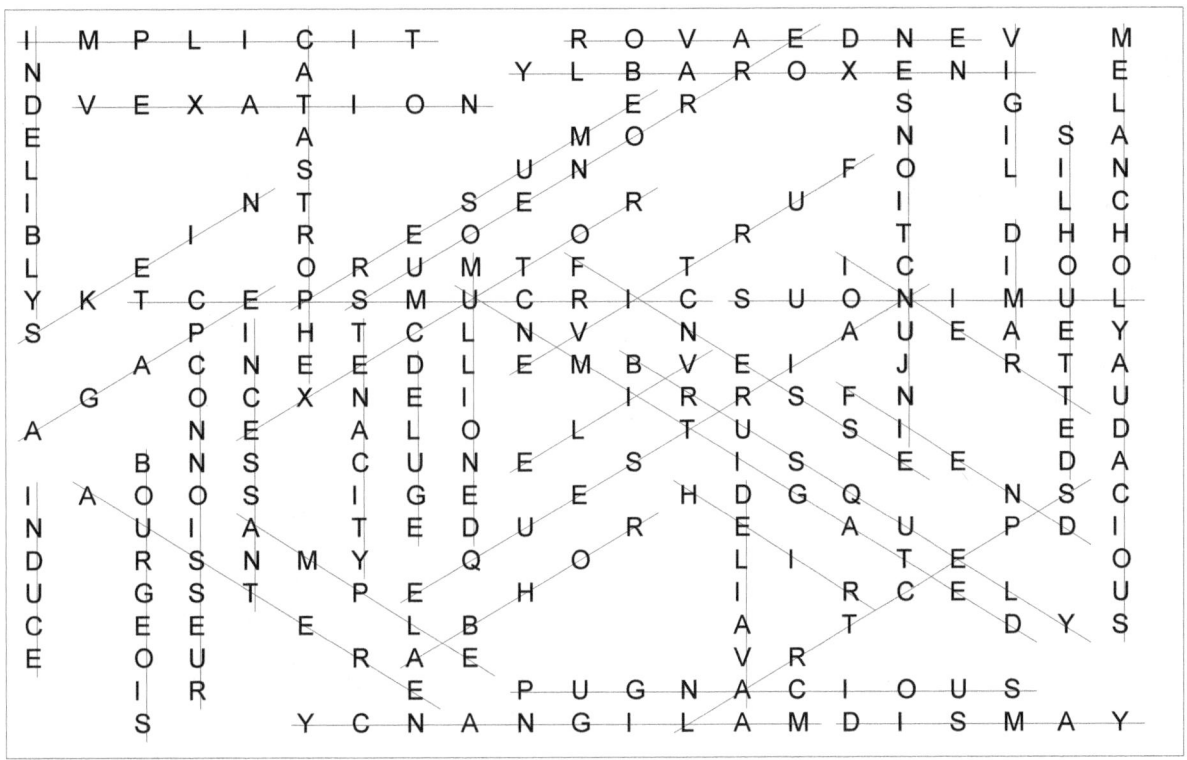

A great, often sudden disaster (11)
A heavy downpour (6)
A person of informed and discriminating taste (11)
Abruptly (9)
Annoyance (8)
Assume; take for granted (7)
Belligerent; has a fighting nature (10)
Constant; continual (9)
Daring; bold (9)
Directives; orders (11)
Emitting light (8)
Enough (5)
Evil (10)
Ghostly (8)
Gloomy (10)
Helped; made use of (7)
Horse or relating to horses (10)
In a state of amazement with the mouth wide open (5)
In the middle of (4)
Influence; persuade (6)
Length of thread or yarn rolled into a loose ball (5)
Loathe; hate (5)
Loathsome; disgusting; objectionable (4)
Looking dark against a light background (11)
Middle class (9)
Mistaken (9)
One who inherits (4)
Period of watchfulness or waiting (5)
Permanently (9)
Perseverance (8)
Person appointed to carry out a will (8)
Prudent; mindful of circumstances (11)
Relentlessly (10)
Skillful, delicate handling (7)
Spirit; demon (5)
Stealthy; sneaky (7)
Stern; somber (7)
Try (8)
Unable to move (5)
Unquestioning (8)
Upset; alarm; disillusion; loss of enthusiasm (6)
With divided panes (9)
Without qualification or exception; absolute (11)

Hound of the Baskervilles Vocabulary Word Search 2

Words are placed backwards, forward, diagonally, up and down. Clues listed below can help you find the words. Circle the hidden vocabulary words in the maze.

```
B Y Q T X F N T L X D M P A X D C B P A E
B L F G M E L P U Q G Z H B K J E A Y M R
W O N X C J J Y M F C D V H A M P L E I R
B H P U G N A C I O U S I O H T E U D O
I C D V J M J N N R Z D L R G U V S M G N
I N J U N C T I O N S R E Y Q I I T A C E
I A C K F C O T U P B H Q S H N T R L L O
C L A E C T U N S C P O U P S E R A I A U
W E G K S C T R N O J R U V P R U D G N S
S M A Y E S O J R O B T R R P T F E N D A
V J P X Q V A T P A I H E C G P Q D A E P
Y I E L A H S N V P U S E N K E H N N S P
W T G E R A I D T E U S S I A B O E C T R
J V D I T M M I W M X Z T E R C N I Y I O
D N X A L U P S E W T A S E U P I F S N B
E G C H B L L M K M J S T W R R B T W E A
L T Q V V L I A P V E W Q I P E S C Y M T
I Z M L W I C Y B N S G D D O M B K Y M I
A K P K N O I T I R A P P A C N J F E C O
V N H Y N N T F C I R C U M S P E C T I N
A C P H J E T P W E Q U E S T R I A N P N
Z B D I N D E L I B L Y S P E C T R A L H
```

A great, often sudden disaster (11)
A heavy downpour (6)
A person of informed and discriminating taste (11)
Abruptly (9)
Annoyance (8)
Assume; take for granted (7)
Belligerent; has a fighting nature (10)
Constant; continual (9)
Directives; orders (11)
Emitting light (8)
Enough (5)
Evil (10)
Ghostly (8)
Ghostly figure (10)
Gloomy (10)
Having a rail supported by posts (11)
Helped; made use of (7)
Horse or relating to horses (10)
In a state of amazement with the mouth wide open (5)
In the middle of (4)
Influence; persuade (6)

Length of thread or yarn rolled into a loose ball (5)
Loathe; hate (5)
Loathsome; disgusting; objectionable (4)
Middle class (9)
Mistaken (9)
Official approval (11)
One who inherits (4)
Period of watchfulness or waiting (5)
Permanently (9)
Perseverance (8)
Person appointed to carry out a will (8)
Prudent; mindful of circumstances (11)
Secret; done in secret (11)
Skillful, delicate handling (7)
Spirit; demon (5)
Stealthy; sneaky (7)
Stern; somber (7)
Try (8)
Unable to move (5)
Unquestioning (8)
Upset; alarm; disillusion; loss of enthusiasm (6)
With divided panes (9)

Hound of the Baskervilles Vocabulary Word Search 2 Answer Key

Words are placed backwards, forward, diagonally, up and down. Clues listed below can help you find the words. Circle the hidden vocabulary words in the maze.

A great, often sudden disaster (11)
A heavy downpour (6)
A person of informed and discriminating taste (11)
Abruptly (9)
Annoyance (8)
Assume; take for granted (7)
Belligerent; has a fighting nature (10)
Constant; continual (9)
Directives; orders (11)
Emitting light (8)
Enough (5)
Evil (10)
Ghostly (8)
Ghostly figure (10)
Gloomy (10)
Having a rail supported by posts (11)
Helped; made use of (7)
Horse or relating to horses (10)
In a state of amazement with the mouth wide open (5)
In the middle of (4)
Influence; persuade (6)

Length of thread or yarn rolled into a loose ball (5)
Loathe; hate (5)
Loathsome; disgusting; objectionable (4)
Middle class (9)
Mistaken (9)
Official approval (11)
One who inherits (4)
Period of watchfulness or waiting (5)
Permanently (9)
Perseverance (8)
Person appointed to carry out a will (8)
Prudent; mindful of circumstances (11)
Secret; done in secret (11)
Skillful, delicate handling (7)
Spirit; demon (5)
Stealthy; sneaky (7)
Stern; somber (7)
Try (8)
Unable to move (5)
Unquestioning (8)
Upset; alarm; disillusion; loss of enthusiasm (6)
With divided panes (9)

Hound of the Baskervilles Vocabulary Word Search 3

Words are placed backwards, forward, diagonally, up and down. Words listed below are included in the maze. Circle the hidden vocabulary words in the maze.

```
A P P R O B A T I O N L V B H V C N N Q V
D C E Q U E S T R I A N E A D T A Y P H K
E B J Q V J C K R R T U X L D M T A B P B
T C O M M U T A T I O N A U M Q A P T J J
T C E P S M U C R I C M T S U P S P S T B
E Y L B I L E D N I W I I T L C T A U K Q
U Y G J L P P C K Z F T O R L Y R R O S T
O D S V S F L Q S Z L I N A I T O I I U Z
H B C P H H Q C E Z N G S D O I P T C O G
L W O J E G Z W Y N L A C E N C H I A N V
I V M U I T L Y J X D T D D E A E O N I T
S H Z X R F U R T I V E C U D N I N G M J
X V L E B G V K T A M D A I Z E V I U U P
Y R N Y C Q E N Y U G P M V Y T L W P L F
H I C E H V A O S A S A L M O Z T U J Y L
V X L Y P S M E I U C R P I R R D W G L Y
C I H D S L R E O S O M S E C E B T R E Q
V W S E P P S E P T Q D H H L I Q F T U L
L D C K F S N P U E A B I I C Z T N S Q W
F N D S E O G C Y R F M A S A B H O R S L
I E V N R I E C J E Q V P D M W D T V U S
H I I R G X N V G L A S R L R A Y W L R B
T F E T E A U D A C I O U S E X Y R V B B
```

ABHOR	BRUSQUELY	FINESSE	PUGNACIOUS
AGAPE	CATASTROPHE	FURTIVE	SILHOUETTED
AMID	CIRCUMSPECT	HEIR	SKEIN
AMPLE	COMMUTATION	IMPLICIT	SPECTRAL
APPARITION	DELUGE	INCESSANT	TENACITY
APPROBATION	DISMAY	INDELIBLY	UNMITIGATED
AUDACIOUS	ENDEAVOR	INDUCE	VEXATION
AUSTERE	EQUESTRIAN	INERT	VIGIL
AVAILED	ERRONEOUS	LUMINOUS	VILE
BALUSTRADED	EXECUTOR	MULLIONED	
BOURGEOIS	FIEND	PRESUME	

Hound of the Baskervilles Vocabulary Word Search 3 Answer Key

Words are placed backwards, forward, diagonally, up and down. Words listed below are included in the maze. Circle the hidden vocabulary words in the maze.

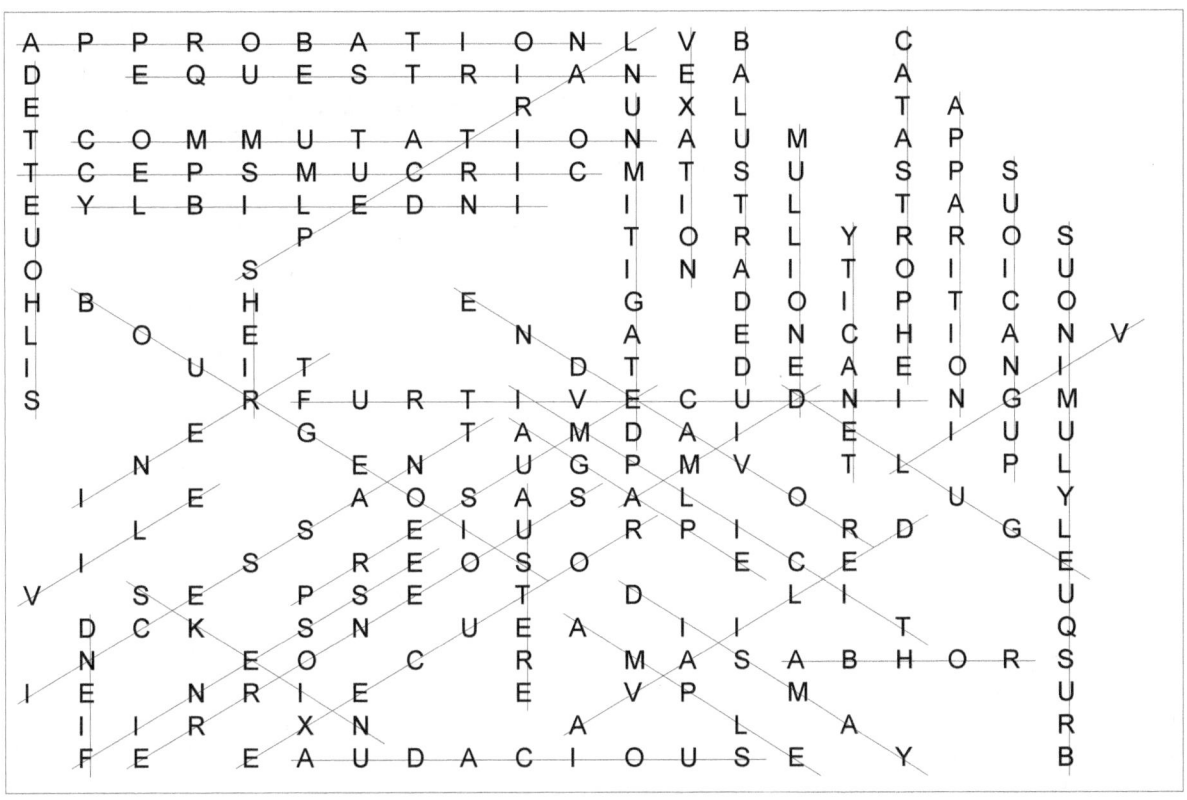

ABHOR	BRUSQUELY	FINESSE	PUGNACIOUS
AGAPE	CATASTROPHE	FURTIVE	SILHOUETTED
AMID	CIRCUMSPECT	HEIR	SKEIN
AMPLE	COMMUTATION	IMPLICIT	SPECTRAL
APPARITION	DELUGE	INCESSANT	TENACITY
APPROBATION	DISMAY	INDELIBLY	UNMITIGATED
AUDACIOUS	ENDEAVOR	INDUCE	VEXATION
AUSTERE	EQUESTRIAN	INERT	VIGIL
AVAILED	ERRONEOUS	LUMINOUS	VILE
BALUSTRADED	EXECUTOR	MULLIONED	
BOURGEOIS	FIEND	PRESUME	

Hound of the Baskervilles Vocabulary Word Search 4

Words are placed backwards, forward, diagonally, up and down. Words listed below are included in the maze. Circle the hidden vocabulary words in the maze.

```
A G A P E L U M I N O U S E F R S R Y C T
R V W G X N B N O I C B C Q J U R K A I E
V P A S J T D I A E H D K U O E C T M N N
F I G I Q E T Q U K J E R E K S A P S C A
X S G L L A X S S S Z N S P S L A I E C I
N J Y I X E Z Q T S Q O S T I K U D S I
X S B E L V D R E R R N D R C O M D K S T
F L V B D D G N R R O E O I Q N F A F A Y
Y I C M J C I S E I D P T A M N Y C C N W
B N T K Y F L L T A H K W N R O K I G T S
O J F I E N D A R E M E L A N C H O L Y I
U U W R G Z T T N N D E N O I L L U M R L
R N F Y N I S K B D D A S J T T B S S P H
G C S G C U H P G E E P P P B W D M D X O
E T G I L K F U D A R S M P E J V I C J U
O I L A N B Q G Z V O D T D A C Q N Q H E
I O B T V D E N Y O T E H I B R T E R V T
S N T G C M U A W R U L Z N N I I R I N T
S S Z N U D A C I R C U M S P E C T A G E
C J H S N M B I E P E G Y H L H R M I L D
G G E R I C H O Y P X E W I C U P D X O M
G R F D S Q O U K K E K V Z F L W P C G N
P B Y R L Z R S B R U S Q U E L Y G S W Y
```

ABHOR	CATASTROPHE	FINESSE	MULLIONED
AGAPE	CIRCUMSPECT	FURTIVE	PRESUME
AMID	CLANDESTINE	HEIR	PUGNACIOUS
AMPLE	CONNOISSEUR	IMPLICIT	SILHOUETTED
APPARITION	DELUGE	INCESSANT	SKEIN
AUDACIOUS	DISMAY	INDELIBLY	SOLICITATIONS
AUSTERE	ENDEAVOR	INDUCE	SPECTRAL
AVAILED	EQUESTRIAN	INERT	TENACITY
BALUSTRADED	ERRONEOUS	INJUNCTIONS	VEXATION
BOURGEOIS	EXECUTOR	LUMINOUS	VIGIL
BRUSQUELY	FIEND	MELANCHOLY	VILE

Copyrighted

Hound of the Baskervilles Vocabulary Word Search 4 Answer Key

Words are placed backwards, forward, diagonally, up and down. Words listed below are included in the maze. Circle the hidden vocabulary words in the maze.

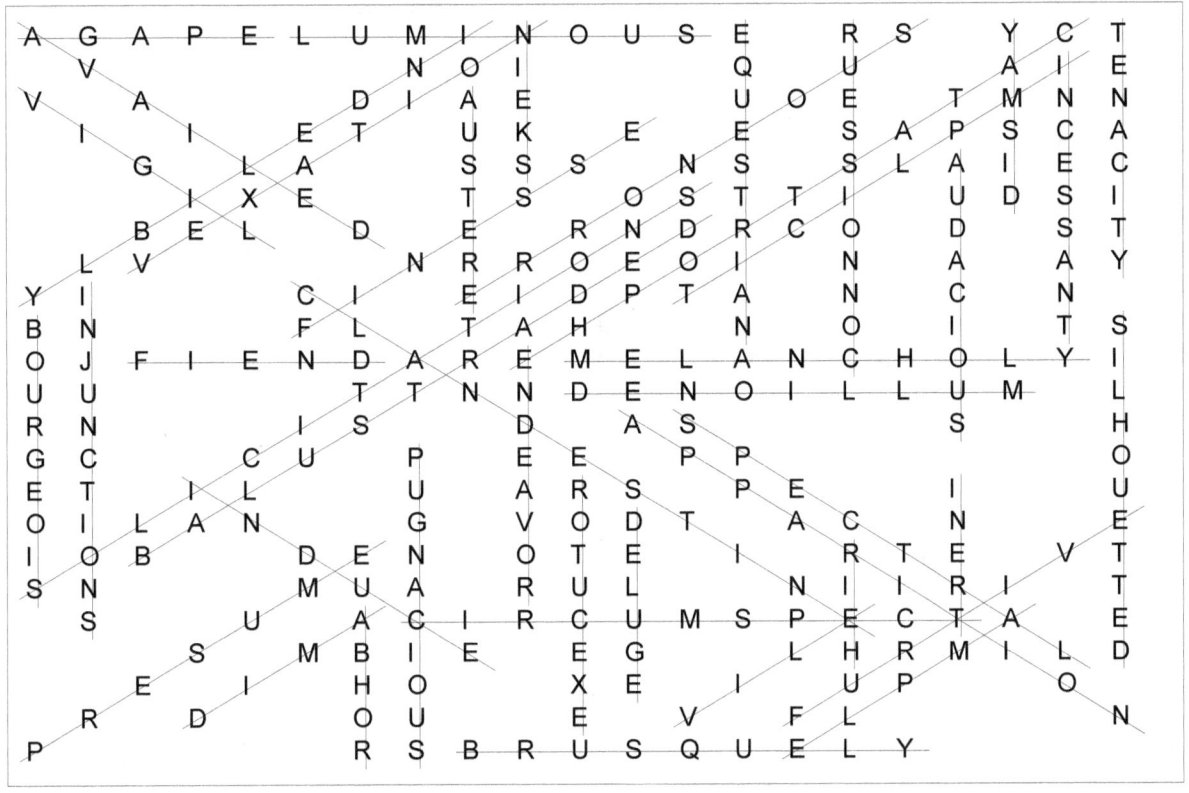

ABHOR	CATASTROPHE	FINESSE	MULLIONED
AGAPE	CIRCUMSPECT	FURTIVE	PRESUME
AMID	CLANDESTINE	HEIR	PUGNACIOUS
AMPLE	CONNOISSEUR	IMPLICIT	SILHOUETTED
APPARITION	DELUGE	INCESSANT	SKEIN
AUDACIOUS	DISMAY	INDELIBLY	SOLICITATIONS
AUSTERE	ENDEAVOR	INDUCE	SPECTRAL
AVAILED	EQUESTRIAN	INERT	TENACITY
BALUSTRADED	ERRONEOUS	INJUNCTIONS	VEXATION
BOURGEOIS	EXECUTOR	LUMINOUS	VIGIL
BRUSQUELY	FIEND	MELANCHOLY	VILE

Hound of the Baskervilles Vocabulary Crossword 1

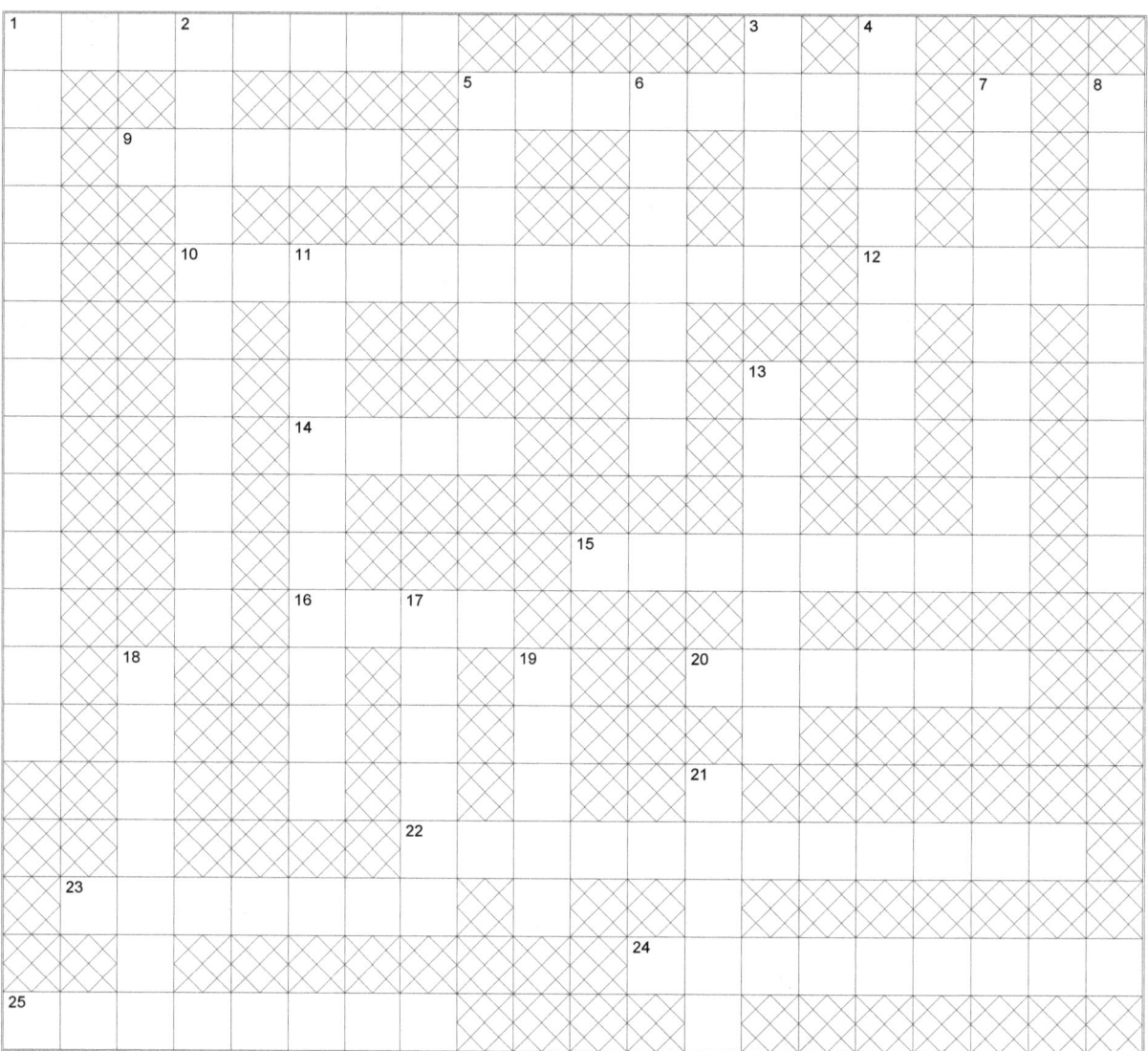

Across
1. Ghostly
5. Annoyance
9. Enough
10. Without qualification or exception; absolute
12. In a state of amazement with the mouth wide open
14. In the middle of
15. Emitting light
16. One who inherits
20. A heavy downpour
22. Supported with other evidence
23. Stealthy; sneaky
24. Middle class
25. Person appointed to carry out a will

Down
1. Pleas; petitions
2. Substitution; exchange
3. Spirit; demon
4. Try
5. Period of watchfulness or waiting
6. Stern; somber
7. Daring; bold
8. Permanently
11. Gloomy
13. Helped; made use of
17. Influence; persuade
18. Assume; take for granted
19. Unable to move
21. Loathe; hate

Hound of the Baskervilles Vocabulary Crossword 1 Answer Key

	1 S	P	2 E C	T	R	A	L				3 F		4 E		
	O		O				5 V	E	X	6 A	T	I	O	N	7 A	8 I
	L		9 A	M	P	L	E		I		U		E		D		U	N
	I		M				G			S		N		E		D		D
	C		10 U	N	11 M	I	T	I	G	A	T	E	D		12 A	G	A	P	E
	I			T		E			L			E			13 V		C		L
	T			A		L					R		A		O		I		I
	A			T		14 A	M	I	D		E			V		R		O		B
	T			I		N							A			U		L
	I			O		C				15 L	U	M	I	N	O	U	S		Y
	O			N		16 H	E	17 I	R				L				
	N		18 P			O		N		19 I		20 D	E	L	U	G	E	
	S		R			L		D		N		D					
			E			Y		U		E		21 A					
			S					22 C	O	R	R	O	B	O	R	A	T	E	D
		23 F	U	R	T	I	V	E		T		H					
			M					24 B	O	U	R	G	E	O	I	S
	25 E	X	E	C	U	T	O	R			R					

Across
1. Ghostly
5. Annoyance
9. Enough
10. Without qualification or exception; absolute
12. In a state of amazement with the mouth wide open
14. In the middle of
15. Emitting light
16. One who inherits
20. A heavy downpour
22. Supported with other evidence
23. Stealthy; sneaky
24. Middle class
25. Person appointed to carry out a will

Down
1. Pleas; petitions
2. Substitution; exchange
3. Spirit; demon
4. Try
5. Period of watchfulness or waiting
6. Stern; somber
7. Daring; bold
8. Permanently
11. Gloomy
13. Helped; made use of
17. Influence; persuade
18. Assume; take for granted
19. Unable to move
21. Loathe; hate

Hound of the Baskervilles Vocabulary Crossword 2

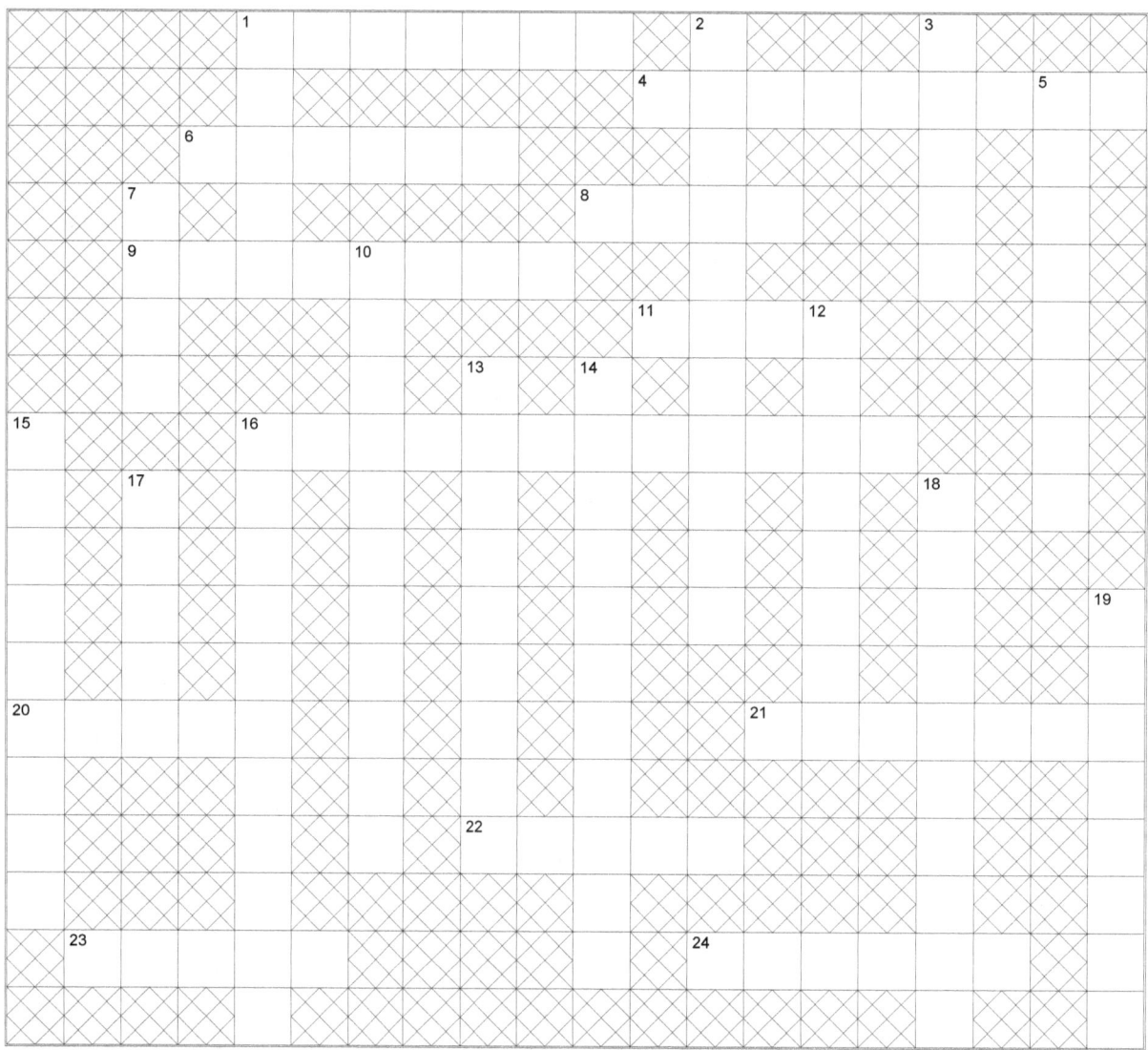

Across
1. Stealthy; sneaky
4. Permanently
6. A heavy downpour
8. In the middle of
9. Try
11. Loathsome; disgusting; objectionable
16. Supported with other evidence
20. Unable to move
21. Assume; take for granted
22. Length of thread or yarn rolled into a loose ball
23. Loathe; hate
24. Upset; alarm; disillusion; loss of enthusiasm

Down
1. Spirit; demon
2. Without qualification or exception; absolute
3. Period of watchfulness or waiting
5. Emitting light
7. One who inherits
10. Official approval
12. Person appointed to carry out a will
13. Middle class
14. A person of informed and discriminating taste
15. Daring; bold
16. Substitution; exchange
17. Enough
18. Horse or relating to horses
19. Ghostly

Hound of the Baskervilles Vocabulary Crossword 2 Answer Key

		1 F	U	R	T	I	V	E		2 U		3 V			
		I						4 I	N	D	E	L	I	B	5 L	Y
	6 D	E	L	U	G	E				M		G		U
	7 H		N				8 A	M	I	D		I		M
	9 E	N	D	10 E	A	V	O	R		T		L		I
	I			P				11 V	I	12 E		N
	R			P		13 B	14 C		G		X		O
15 A		16 C	O	R	R	O	B	O	R	A	T	E	D		U
U		17 A	O	O		U	N		T		C		18 E	S
D		M	M	B		R	N		E		U		Q
A		P	M	A		G	O		D		T		U		19 S
C		L	U	T		E	I				O		E		P
20 I	N	E	R	T		I	O	S		21 P	R	E	S	U	M	E
O			A	O		I	S				T				C
U			T	N		22 S	K	E	I	N		R		T
S			I					U				I		R
	23 A	B	H	O	R			R		24 D	I	S	M	A	Y	A
			N									N		L

Across
1. Stealthy; sneaky
4. Permanently
6. A heavy downpour
8. In the middle of
9. Try
11. Loathsome; disgusting; objectionable
16. Supported with other evidence
20. Unable to move
21. Assume; take for granted
22. Length of thread or yarn rolled into a loose ball
23. Loathe; hate
24. Upset; alarm; disillusion; loss of enthusiasm

Down
1. Spirit; demon
2. Without qualification or exception; absolute
3. Period of watchfulness or waiting
5. Emitting light
7. One who inherits
10. Official approval
12. Person appointed to carry out a will
13. Middle class
14. A person of informed and discriminating taste
15. Daring; bold
16. Substitution; exchange
17. Enough
18. Horse or relating to horses
19. Ghostly

Hound of the Baskervilles Vocabulary Crossword 3

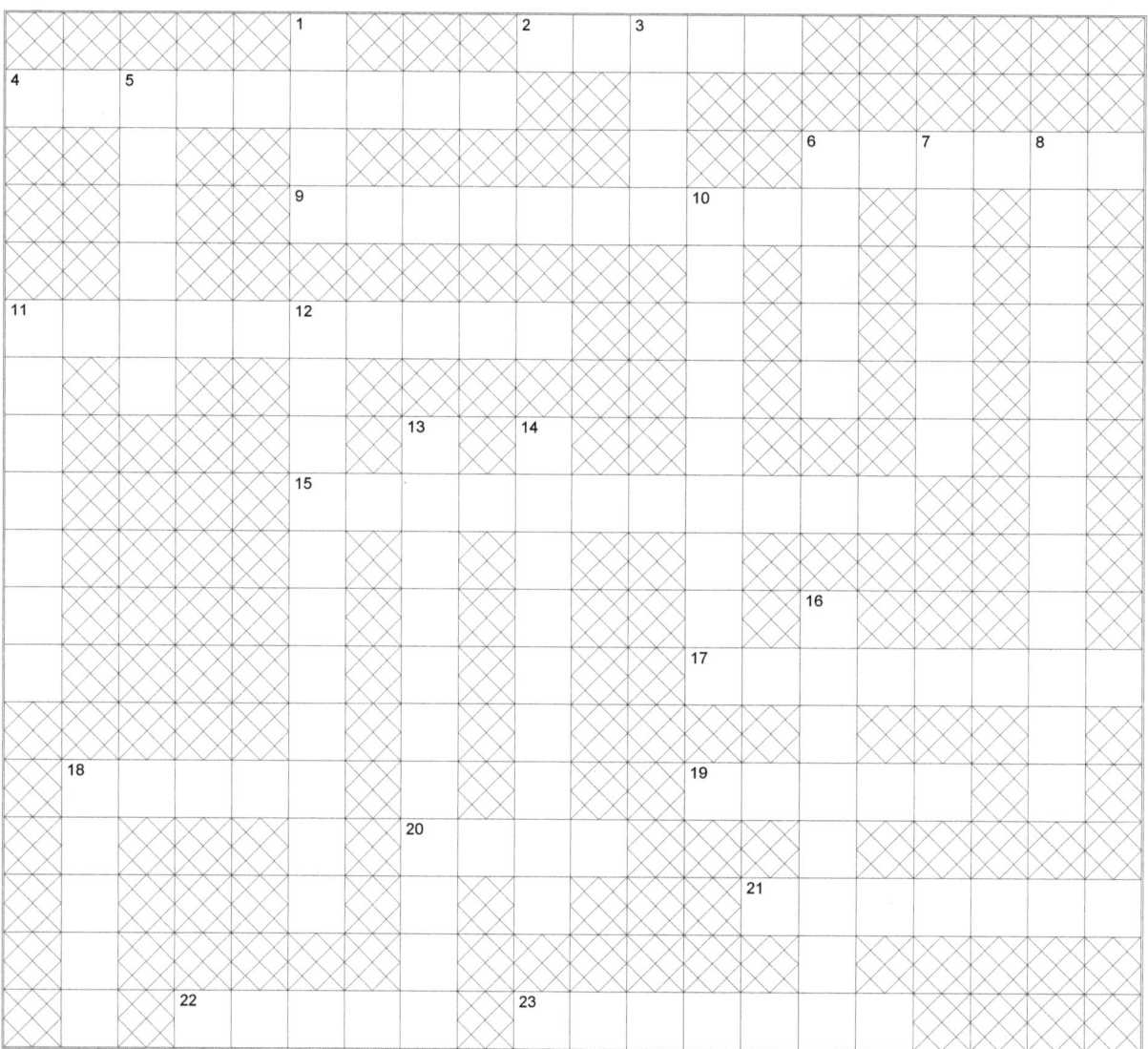

Across
2. Loathe; hate
4. Daring; bold
6. Influence; persuade
9. Horse or relating to horses
11. Belligerent; has a fighting nature
15. A person of informed and discriminating taste
17. Perseverance
18. Enough
19. Length of thread or yarn rolled into a loose ball
20. In the middle of
21. Helped; made use of
22. Spirit; demon
23. Stern; somber

Down
1. Loathsome; disgusting; objectionable
3. One who inherits
5. A heavy downpour
6. Unable to move
7. Upset; alarm; disillusion; loss of enthusiasm
8. Supported with other evidence
10. Constant; continual
11. Assume; take for granted
12. Prudent; mindful of circumstances
13. Without qualification or exception; absolute
14. Middle class
16. Try
18. In a state of amazement with the mouth wide open

Hound of the Baskervilles Vocabulary Crossword 3 Answer Key

Across
2. Loathe; hate
4. Daring; bold
6. Influence; persuade
9. Horse or relating to horses
11. Belligerent; has a fighting nature
15. A person of informed and discriminating taste
17. Perseverance
18. Enough
19. Length of thread or yarn rolled into a loose ball
20. In the middle of
21. Helped; made use of
22. Spirit; demon
23. Stern; somber

Down
1. Loathsome; disgusting; objectionable
3. One who inherits
5. A heavy downpour
6. Unable to move
7. Upset; alarm; disillusion; loss of enthusiasm
8. Supported with other evidence
10. Constant; continual
11. Assume; take for granted
12. Prudent; mindful of circumstances
13. Without qualification or exception; absolute
14. Middle class
16. Try
18. In a state of amazement with the mouth wide open

Hound of the Baskervilles Vocabulary Crossword 4

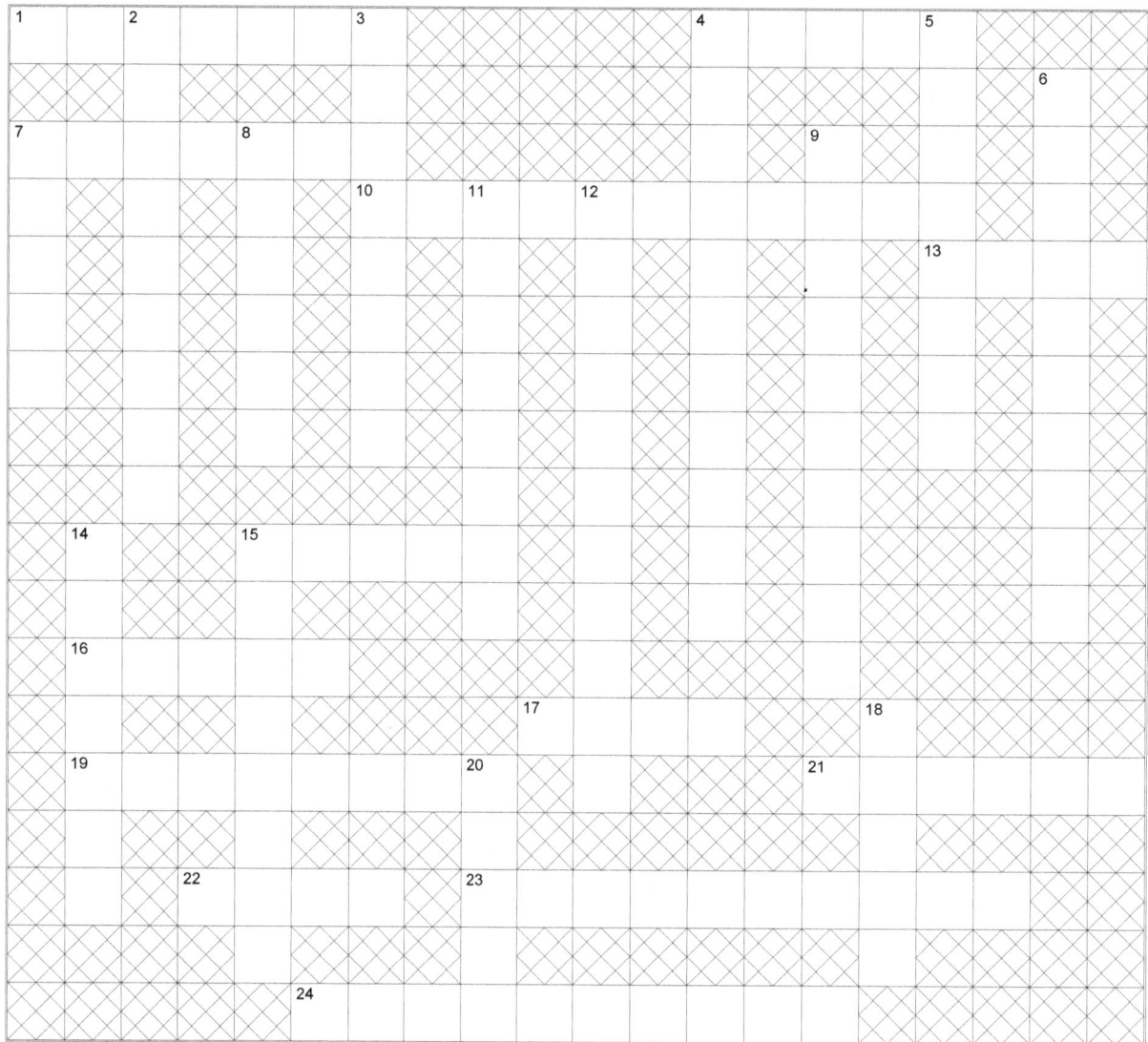

Across
1. Assume; take for granted
4. Enough
7. Stealthy; sneaky
10. A great, often sudden disaster
13. In the middle of
15. Unable to move
16. In a state of amazement with the mouth wide open
17. One who inherits
19. Emitting light
21. Upset; alarm; disillusion; loss of enthusiasm
22. Loathsome; disgusting; objectionable
23. Horse or relating to horses
24. Belligerent; has a fighting nature

Down
2. Mistaken
3. Person appointed to carry out a will
4. Official approval
5. Try
6. Evil
7. Spirit; demon
8. Influence; persuade
9. Ghostly figure
11. Perseverance
12. Looking dark against a light background
14. Helped; made use of
15. Unquestioning
18. Period of watchfulness or waiting
20. Length of thread or yarn rolled into a loose ball

Hound of the Baskervilles Vocabulary Crossword 4 Answer Key

	1	2	3	4	5	6	7	8	9	10	11	12	13
1	P	R	E	S	U	M	E			A	M	P	L	E
			R			X				P			N		M
7	F	U	R	T	I	V	E			P		A		D		A
	I		O		N		10 C	A	T	A	S	T	R	O	P	H	E	L
	E		N		D		U		T	E		I		O	P		13 A	M	I	D
	N		E		U		T		N		L		B		A		V		G
	D		O		C		O		A		H		A		R		O		N
			U		E		R		C		O		T		I		R		A
			S						I		U		I		T				N
		14 A		15 I	N	E	R	T		E		O		I				C
		V		M				Y		T		N		O				Y
		16 A	G	A	P	E				T				N				
		I		L				17 H	E	I	R		18 V		
		19 L	U	M	I	N	O	U	S		20 S		D		21 D	I	S	M	A	Y
		E		C						K			G	
		D		22 V	I	L	E		23 E	Q	U	E	S	T	R	I	A	N
				T				I				L
				24 P	U	G	N	A	C	I	O	U	S

Across
1. Assume; take for granted
4. Enough
7. Stealthy; sneaky
10. A great, often sudden disaster
13. In the middle of
15. Unable to move
16. In a state of amazement with the mouth wide open
17. One who inherits
19. Emitting light
21. Upset; alarm; disillusion; loss of enthusiasm
22. Loathsome; disgusting; objectionable
23. Horse or relating to horses
24. Belligerent; has a fighting nature

Down
2. Mistaken
3. Person appointed to carry out a will
4. Official approval
5. Try
6. Evil
7. Spirit; demon
8. Influence; persuade
9. Ghostly figure
11. Perseverance
12. Looking dark against a light background
14. Helped; made use of
15. Unquestioning
18. Period of watchfulness or waiting
20. Length of thread or yarn rolled into a loose ball

Hound of the Baskervilles Vocabulary Juggle Letters 1

1. LIVGI = 1. _____
Period of watchfulness or waiting

2. EDEOSTTUHLI = 2. _____
Looking dark against a light background

3. ATIRENUSEQ = 3. _____
Horse or relating to horses

4. RUIFTEV = 4. _____
Stealthy; sneaky

5. EIRH = 5. _____
One who inherits

6. GUOBSOIER = 6. _____
Middle class

7. DNIEF = 7. _____
Spirit; demon

8. PLMAE = 8. _____
Enough

9. ACNTMTIUMOO = 9. _____
Substitution; exchange

10. CIEANTTY =10. _____
Perseverance

11. NTECSINAS =11. _____
Constant; continual

12. UCCTMISPREC =12. _____
Prudent; mindful of circumstances

13. SATOTLINICOSI =13. _____
Pleas; petitions

14. TUASLRBADED =14. _____
Having a rail supported by posts

15. IAUNOUSPCG =15. _____
Belligerent; has a fighting nature

Hound of the Baskervilles Vocabulary Juggle Letters 1 Answer Key

1. LIVGI = 1. VIGIL
   Period of watchfulness or waiting

2. EDEOSTTUHLI = 2. SILHOUETTED
   Looking dark against a light background

3. ATIRENUSEQ = 3. EQUESTRIAN
   Horse or relating to horses

4. RUIFTEV = 4. FURTIVE
   Stealthy; sneaky

5. EIRH = 5. HEIR
   One who inherits

6. GUOBSOIER = 6. BOURGEOIS
   Middle class

7. DNIEF = 7. FIEND
   Spirit; demon

8. PLMAE = 8. AMPLE
   Enough

9. ACNTMTIUMOO = 9. COMMUTATION
   Substitution; exchange

10. CIEANTTY = 10. TENACITY
    Perseverance

11. NTECSINAS = 11. INCESSANT
    Constant; continual

12. UCCTMISPREC = 12. CIRCUMSPECT
    Prudent; mindful of circumstances

13. SATOTLINICOSI = 13. SOLICITATIONS
    Pleas; petitions

14. TUASLRBADED = 14. BALUSTRADED
    Having a rail supported by posts

15. IAUNOUSPCG = 15. PUGNACIOUS
    Belligerent; has a fighting nature

Hound of the Baskervilles Vocabulary Juggle Letters 2

1. ULSUIMNO = 1. _____
   Emitting light

2. ONNSRCSUOEI = 2. _____
   A person of informed and discriminating taste

3. EDNFI = 3. _____
   Spirit; demon

4. IEXATNVO = 4. _____
   Annoyance

5. GYINALMCNA = 5. _____
   Evil

6. ITCOMMUOTAN = 6. _____
   Substitution; exchange

7. RENOUSOER = 7. _____
   Mistaken

8. EKNSI = 8. _____
   Length of thread or yarn rolled into a loose ball

9. IUTEANQESR = 9. _____
   Horse or relating to horses

10. LEINTADENCS = 10. _____
    Secret; done in secret

11. PCEALSTR = 11. _____
    Ghostly

12. EAPGA = 12. _____
    In a state of amazement with the mouth wide open

13. UNUSACGOPI = 13. _____
    Belligerent; has a fighting nature

14. TJONSUINNIC = 14. _____
    Directives; orders

15. INEESSF = 15. _____
    Skillful, delicate handling

Hound of the Baskervilles Vocabulary Juggle Letters 2 Answer Key

1. ULSUIMNO = 1. LUMINOUS
   Emitting light

2. ONNSRCSUOEI = 2. CONNOISSEUR
   A person of informed and discriminating taste

3. EDNFI = 3. FIEND
   Spirit; demon

4. IEXATNVO = 4. VEXATION
   Annoyance

5. GYINALMCNA = 5. MALIGNANCY
   Evil

6. ITCOMMUOTAN = 6. COMMUTATION
   Substitution; exchange

7. RENOUSOER = 7. ERRONEOUS
   Mistaken

8. EKNSI = 8. SKEIN
   Length of thread or yarn rolled into a loose ball

9. IUTEANQESR = 9. EQUESTRIAN
   Horse or relating to horses

10. LEINTADENCS = 10. CLANDESTINE
    Secret; done in secret

11. PCEALSTR = 11. SPECTRAL
    Ghostly

12. EAPGA = 12. AGAPE
    In a state of amazement with the mouth wide open

13. UNUSACGOPI = 13. PUGNACIOUS
    Belligerent; has a fighting nature

14. TJONSUINNIC = 14. INJUNCTIONS
    Directives; orders

15. INEESSF = 15. FINESSE
    Skillful, delicate handling

Hound of the Baskervilles Vocabulary Juggle Letters 3

1. CENDUI = 1. _____
   Influence; persuade

2. SUUACADIO = 2. _____
   Daring; bold

3. TONISOIILCATS = 3. _____
   Pleas; petitions

4. NSESEIF = 4. _____
   Skillful, delicate handling

5. IPCUCMRESCT = 5. _____
   Prudent; mindful of circumstances

6. AYTNTCEI = 6. _____
   Perseverance

7. LEDUEG = 7. _____
   A heavy downpour

8. STRUAEE = 8. _____
   Stern; somber

9. ITNEVXOA = 9. _____
   Annoyance

10. EFDNI = 10. _____
    Spirit; demon

11. EOSONRREU = 11. _____
    Mistaken

12. TNPBIPAROAO = 12. _____
    Official approval

13. LPAME = 13. _____
    Enough

14. CAPUINUOGS = 14. _____
    Belligerent; has a fighting nature

15. DALAIEV = 15. _____
    Helped; made use of

Hound of the Baskervilles Vocabulary Juggle Letters 3 Answer Key

1. CENDUI = 1. INDUCE
Influence; persuade

2. SUUACADIO = 2. AUDACIOUS
Daring; bold

3. TONISOIILCATS = 3. SOLICITATIONS
Pleas; petitions

4. NSESEIF = 4. FINESSE
Skillful, delicate handling

5. IPCUCMRESCT = 5. CIRCUMSPECT
Prudent; mindful of circumstances

6. AYTNTCEI = 6. TENACITY
Perseverance

7. LEDUEG = 7. DELUGE
A heavy downpour

8. STRUAEE = 8. AUSTERE
Stern; somber

9. ITNEVXOA = 9. VEXATION
Annoyance

10. EFDNI =10. FIEND
Spirit; demon

11. EOSONRREU =11. ERRONEOUS
Mistaken

12. TNPBIPAROAO =12. APPROBATION
Official approval

13. LPAME =13. AMPLE
Enough

14. CAPUINUOGS =14. PUGNACIOUS
Belligerent; has a fighting nature

15. DALAIEV =15. AVAILED
Helped; made use of

Hound of the Baskervilles Vocabulary Juggle Letters 4

1. DTABRORORECO = 1. _____
   Supported with other evidence

2. IENTR = 2. _____
   Unable to move

3. SSNCURIOENO = 3. _____
   A person of informed and discriminating taste

4. PEAGA = 4. _____
   In a state of amazement with the mouth wide open

5. IPBOTOPNRAA = 5. _____
   Official approval

6. LRTEAPCS = 6. _____
   Ghostly

7. RTEOSPACHAT = 7. _____
   A great, often sudden disaster

8. EVIL = 8. _____
   Loathsome; disgusting; objectionable

9. IGVIL = 9. _____
   Period of watchfulness or waiting

10. EULDGE = 10. _____
    A heavy downpour

11. SBADUADRLTE = 11. _____
    Having a rail supported by posts

12. RCTEUXEO = 12. _____
    Person appointed to carry out a will

13. DCNEUI = 13. _____
    Influence; persuade

14. EDIFN = 14. _____
    Spirit; demon

15. IKSNE = 15. _____
    Length of thread or yarn rolled into a loose ball

Hound of the Baskervilles Vocabulary Juggle Letters 4 Answer Key

1. DTABROROREDO = 1. CORROBORATED
Supported with other evidence

2. IENTR = 2. INERT
Unable to move

3. SSNCURIOENO = 3. CONNOISSEUR
A person of informed and discriminating taste

4. PEAGA = 4. AGAPE
In a state of amazement with the mouth wide open

5. IPBOTOPNRAA = 5. APPROBATION
Official approval

6. LRTEAPCS = 6. SPECTRAL
Ghostly

7. RTEOSPACHAT = 7. CATASTROPHE
A great, often sudden disaster

8. EVIL = 8. VILE
Loathsome; disgusting; objectionable

9. IGVIL = 9. VIGIL
Period of watchfulness or waiting

10. EULDGE = 10. DELUGE
A heavy downpour

11. SBADUADRLTE = 11. BALUSTRADED
Having a rail supported by posts

12. RCTEUXEO = 12. EXECUTOR
Person appointed to carry out a will

13. DCNEUI = 13. INDUCE
Influence; persuade

14. EDIFN = 14. FIEND
Spirit; demon

15. IKSNE = 15. SKEIN
Length of thread or yarn rolled into a loose ball

ABHOR	Loathe; hate
AGAPE	In a state of amazement with the mouth wide open
AMID	In the middle of
AMPLE	Enough
APPARITION	Ghostly figure
APPROBATION	Official approval
AUDACIOUS	Daring; bold

AUSTERE	Stern; somber
AVAILED	Helped; made use of
BALUSTRADED	Having a rail supported by posts
BOURGEOIS	Middle class
BRUSQUELY	Abruptly
CATASTROPHE	A great, often sudden disaster
CIRCUMSPECT	Prudent; mindful of circumstances

CLANDESTINE	Secret; done in secret
COMMUTATION	Substitution; exchange
CONNOISSEUR	A person of informed and discriminating taste
CORROBORATED	Supported with other evidence
DELUGE	A heavy downpour
DISMAY	Upset; alarm; disillusion; loss of enthusiasm
ENDEAVOR	Try

EQUESTRIAN	Horse or relating to horses
ERRONEOUS	Mistaken
EXECUTOR	Person appointed to carry out a will
FIEND	Spirit; demon
FINESSE	Skillful, delicate handling
FURTIVE	Stealthy; sneaky
HEIR	One who inherits

IMPLICIT	Unquestioning
INCESSANT	Constant; continual
INDELIBLY	Permanently
INDUCE	Influence; persuade
INERT	Unable to move
INEXORABLY	Relentlessly
INJUNCTIONS	Directives; orders

LUMINOUS	Emitting light
MALIGNANCY	Evil
MELANCHOLY	Gloomy
MULLIONED	With divided panes
PRESUME	Assume; take for granted
PUGNACIOUS	Belligerent; has a fighting nature
SILHOUETTED	Looking dark against a light background

SKEIN	Length of thread or yarn rolled into a loose ball
SOLICITATIONS	Pleas; petitions
SPECTRAL	Ghostly
TENACITY	Perseverance
UNMITIGATED	Without qualification or exception; absolute
VEXATION	Annoyance
VIGIL	Period of watchfulness or waiting

VILE	Loathsome; disgusting; objectionable

Hound of the Baskervilles Vocabulary

MULLIONED	CIRCUMSPECT	DELUGE	BALUSTRADED	VIGIL
INJUNCTIONS	CONNOISSEUR	AMID	SKEIN	VEXATION
PRESUME	CLANDESTINE	FREE SPACE	SOLICITATIONS	APPROBATION
EQUESTRIAN	FIEND	LUMINOUS	UNMITIGATED	SPECTRAL
AMPLE	INERT	CORROBORATED	ERRONEOUS	DISMAY

Hound of the Baskervilles Vocabulary

MALIGNANCY	AVAILED	FURTIVE	ENDEAVOR	BRUSQUELY
AUSTERE	COMMUTATION	AGAPE	HEIR	CATASTROPHE
INDELIBLY	TENACITY	FREE SPACE	ABHOR	IMPLICIT
BOURGEOIS	VILE	EXECUTOR	SILHOUETTED	INDUCE
INEXORABLY	APPARITION	MELANCHOLY	PUGNACIOUS	INCESSANT

Hound of the Baskervilles Vocabulary

PUGNACIOUS	CATASTROPHE	INJUNCTIONS	BALUSTRADED	IMPLICIT
COMMUTATION	CORROBORATED	SPECTRAL	APPARITION	FURTIVE
EXECUTOR	AMPLE	FREE SPACE	CIRCUMSPECT	AMID
AVAILED	CONNOISSEUR	DISMAY	FIEND	INEXORABLY
MELANCHOLY	APPROBATION	ENDEAVOR	VIGIL	AUDACIOUS

Hound of the Baskervilles Vocabulary

SKEIN	MALIGNANCY	LUMINOUS	DELUGE	UNMITIGATED
INCESSANT	SILHOUETTED	INDELIBLY	EQUESTRIAN	TENACITY
FINESSE	PRESUME	FREE SPACE	VILE	MULLIONED
INDUCE	ERRONEOUS	SOLICITATIONS	AGAPE	VEXATION
INERT	HEIR	ABHOR	BRUSQUELY	AUSTERE

Hound of the Baskervilles Vocabulary

FURTIVE	AMID	MELANCHOLY	CATASTROPHE	IMPLICIT
ENDEAVOR	APPROBATION	EXECUTOR	INDELIBLY	UNMITIGATED
INDUCE	HEIR	FREE SPACE	INERT	DELUGE
BOURGEOIS	ABHOR	APPARITION	TENACITY	SPECTRAL
VIGIL	PUGNACIOUS	AVAILED	CORROBORATED	AMPLE

Hound of the Baskervilles Vocabulary

BALUSTRADED	AGAPE	INCESSANT	VILE	CLANDESTINE
CONNOISSEUR	AUDACIOUS	PRESUME	MULLIONED	LUMINOUS
BRUSQUELY	SILHOUETTED	FREE SPACE	EQUESTRIAN	INEXORABLY
DISMAY	VEXATION	SOLICITATIONS	COMMUTATION	ERRONEOUS
FINESSE	CIRCUMSPECT	INJUNCTIONS	MALIGNANCY	FIEND

Hound of the Baskervilles Vocabulary

MULLIONED	INERT	INDELIBLY	EQUESTRIAN	AUDACIOUS
CONNOISSEUR	COMMUTATION	UNMITIGATED	MALIGNANCY	CATASTROPHE
PRESUME	VEXATION	FREE SPACE	INDUCE	AGAPE
BALUSTRADED	ERRONEOUS	SOLICITATIONS	BOURGEOIS	AMID
APPARITION	CLANDESTINE	SPECTRAL	VIGIL	DELUGE

Hound of the Baskervilles Vocabulary

AUSTERE	AMPLE	TENACITY	EXECUTOR	DISMAY
SKEIN	ENDEAVOR	LUMINOUS	CIRCUMSPECT	INJUNCTIONS
FIEND	VILE	FREE SPACE	INEXORABLY	AVAILED
IMPLICIT	PUGNACIOUS	FURTIVE	SILHOUETTED	BRUSQUELY
ABHOR	CORROBORATED	APPROBATION	HEIR	FINESSE

Hound of the Baskervilles Vocabulary

HEIR	MULLIONED	COMMUTATION	AGAPE	AUDACIOUS
DISMAY	MALIGNANCY	EXECUTOR	MELANCHOLY	PRESUME
CIRCUMSPECT	CLANDESTINE	FREE SPACE	IMPLICIT	PUGNACIOUS
INERT	BOURGEOIS	INJUNCTIONS	EQUESTRIAN	FINESSE
SILHOUETTED	VILE	VIGIL	CONNOISSEUR	SKEIN

Hound of the Baskervilles Vocabulary

BALUSTRADED	CATASTROPHE	AMID	ENDEAVOR	INEXORABLY
ABHOR	INDUCE	INDELIBLY	CORROBORATED	AMPLE
APPARITION	APPROBATION	FREE SPACE	SOLICITATIONS	INCESSANT
UNMITIGATED	TENACITY	AVAILED	AUSTERE	ERRONEOUS
LUMINOUS	FIEND	BRUSQUELY	FURTIVE	VEXATION

Hound of the Baskervilles Vocabulary

DISMAY	AMID	LUMINOUS	FURTIVE	MULLIONED
ENDEAVOR	SILHOUETTED	AMPLE	ERRONEOUS	AUSTERE
INCESSANT	VIGIL	FREE SPACE	PUGNACIOUS	APPARITION
UNMITIGATED	IMPLICIT	SPECTRAL	APPROBATION	AUDACIOUS
CORROBORATED	INDELIBLY	FINESSE	BRUSQUELY	AVAILED

Hound of the Baskervilles Vocabulary

INERT	CIRCUMSPECT	DELUGE	EXECUTOR	SKEIN
BOURGEOIS	VEXATION	TENACITY	PRESUME	MALIGNANCY
FIEND	HEIR	FREE SPACE	AGAPE	VILE
CLANDESTINE	INDUCE	MELANCHOLY	ABHOR	CONNOISSEUR
SOLICITATIONS	INEXORABLY	COMMUTATION	CATASTROPHE	INJUNCTIONS

Hound of the Baskervilles Vocabulary

UNMITIGATED	ENDEAVOR	INEXORABLY	CIRCUMSPECT	DELUGE
SKEIN	SOLICITATIONS	EQUESTRIAN	FURTIVE	CONNOISSEUR
VIGIL	SILHOUETTED	FREE SPACE	INCESSANT	PRESUME
ABHOR	INERT	MALIGNANCY	FIEND	DISMAY
VEXATION	INDUCE	AVAILED	AMPLE	SPECTRAL

Hound of the Baskervilles Vocabulary

LUMINOUS	HEIR	COMMUTATION	APPROBATION	INDELIBLY
AUDACIOUS	MELANCHOLY	MULLIONED	VILE	AGAPE
BALUSTRADED	INJUNCTIONS	FREE SPACE	TENACITY	FINESSE
PUGNACIOUS	AMID	IMPLICIT	ERRONEOUS	BRUSQUELY
BOURGEOIS	CLANDESTINE	AUSTERE	CATASTROPHE	CORROBORATED

Hound of the Baskervilles Vocabulary

SKEIN	HEIR	CATASTROPHE	MALIGNANCY	INEXORABLY
IMPLICIT	FURTIVE	BOURGEOIS	ENDEAVOR	AUSTERE
VILE	MELANCHOLY	FREE SPACE	DISMAY	EQUESTRIAN
ERRONEOUS	INDELIBLY	CLANDESTINE	EXECUTOR	SOLICITATIONS
INJUNCTIONS	APPARITION	SPECTRAL	AMID	PUGNACIOUS

Hound of the Baskervilles Vocabulary

MULLIONED	VEXATION	CORROBORATED	AGAPE	FIEND
SILHOUETTED	TENACITY	FINESSE	INCESSANT	BRUSQUELY
INDUCE	INERT	FREE SPACE	AVAILED	VIGIL
APPROBATION	CONNOISSEUR	AUDACIOUS	UNMITIGATED	LUMINOUS
AMPLE	PRESUME	ABHOR	DELUGE	COMMUTATION

Hound of the Baskervilles Vocabulary

ENDEAVOR	BALUSTRADED	SPECTRAL	FURTIVE	CATASTROPHE
LUMINOUS	AMID	COMMUTATION	MULLIONED	APPROBATION
APPARITION	BRUSQUELY	FREE SPACE	AUSTERE	CLANDESTINE
VILE	SILHOUETTED	PRESUME	INERT	DELUGE
AGAPE	INJUNCTIONS	AMPLE	ABHOR	VEXATION

Hound of the Baskervilles Vocabulary

FINESSE	EQUESTRIAN	IMPLICIT	CIRCUMSPECT	INCESSANT
AUDACIOUS	BOURGEOIS	AVAILED	MELANCHOLY	TENACITY
EXECUTOR	FIEND	FREE SPACE	MALIGNANCY	PUGNACIOUS
CONNOISSEUR	DISMAY	HEIR	SKEIN	INDELIBLY
VIGIL	ERRONEOUS	CORROBORATED	INDUCE	INEXORABLY

Hound of the Baskervilles Vocabulary

PRESUME	BRUSQUELY	VEXATION	AUSTERE	INCESSANT
ERRONEOUS	BALUSTRADED	AGAPE	PUGNACIOUS	AMPLE
INERT	CLANDESTINE	FREE SPACE	CORROBORATED	LUMINOUS
SPECTRAL	AUDACIOUS	INEXORABLY	APPARITION	COMMUTATION
CIRCUMSPECT	ABHOR	MALIGNANCY	AVAILED	INDELIBLY

Hound of the Baskervilles Vocabulary

BOURGEOIS	CATASTROPHE	EXECUTOR	VIGIL	TENACITY
FINESSE	SILHOUETTED	DELUGE	INDUCE	HEIR
INJUNCTIONS	AMID	FREE SPACE	ENDEAVOR	UNMITIGATED
FURTIVE	FIEND	DISMAY	IMPLICIT	CONNOISSEUR
EQUESTRIAN	SOLICITATIONS	APPROBATION	SKEIN	MULLIONED

Hound of the Baskervilles Vocabulary

AUSTERE	LUMINOUS	SPECTRAL	MALIGNANCY	IMPLICIT
FIEND	FURTIVE	AUDACIOUS	VEXATION	CLANDESTINE
ERRONEOUS	AGAPE	FREE SPACE	INCESSANT	TENACITY
INDUCE	UNMITIGATED	PRESUME	SKEIN	APPARITION
CONNOISSEUR	EQUESTRIAN	CIRCUMSPECT	INEXORABLY	ENDEAVOR

Hound of the Baskervilles Vocabulary

VILE	AMPLE	SOLICITATIONS	PUGNACIOUS	HEIR
FINESSE	AMID	MULLIONED	APPROBATION	MELANCHOLY
COMMUTATION	BRUSQUELY	FREE SPACE	INDELIBLY	SILHOUETTED
BALUSTRADED	VIGIL	DELUGE	ABHOR	INERT
DISMAY	INJUNCTIONS	AVAILED	CORROBORATED	EXECUTOR

Hound of the Baskervilles Vocabulary

VILE	DISMAY	CONNOISSEUR	PUGNACIOUS	IMPLICIT
FINESSE	EXECUTOR	AMPLE	INDUCE	INCESSANT
MULLIONED	AUSTERE	FREE SPACE	INERT	MALIGNANCY
ERRONEOUS	VIGIL	APPROBATION	SILHOUETTED	ENDEAVOR
AGAPE	MELANCHOLY	SPECTRAL	INDELIBLY	EQUESTRIAN

Hound of the Baskervilles Vocabulary

TENACITY	DELUGE	AUDACIOUS	LUMINOUS	ABHOR
CIRCUMSPECT	CORROBORATED	SOLICITATIONS	HEIR	BRUSQUELY
COMMUTATION	APPARITION	FREE SPACE	CATASTROPHE	CLANDESTINE
UNMITIGATED	BALUSTRADED	AMID	BOURGEOIS	VEXATION
FURTIVE	INEXORABLY	SKEIN	FIEND	PRESUME

Hound of the Baskervilles Vocabulary

PUGNACIOUS	VEXATION	INERT	INEXORABLY	MULLIONED
CIRCUMSPECT	AUDACIOUS	AVAILED	UNMITIGATED	CONNOISSEUR
CATASTROPHE	DISMAY	FREE SPACE	INDELIBLY	TENACITY
FINESSE	FIEND	PRESUME	VIGIL	APPARITION
LUMINOUS	IMPLICIT	INDUCE	AMPLE	SPECTRAL

Hound of the Baskervilles Vocabulary

ERRONEOUS	ENDEAVOR	FURTIVE	CLANDESTINE	SILHOUETTED
SKEIN	APPROBATION	AGAPE	INCESSANT	HEIR
ABHOR	COMMUTATION	FREE SPACE	EXECUTOR	EQUESTRIAN
INJUNCTIONS	AUSTERE	CORROBORATED	DELUGE	VILE
BOURGEOIS	AMID	SOLICITATIONS	MALIGNANCY	BRUSQUELY

Hound of the Baskervilles Vocabulary

ERRONEOUS	IMPLICIT	APPROBATION	AMID	EQUESTRIAN
PRESUME	SPECTRAL	COMMUTATION	EXECUTOR	AUDACIOUS
BALUSTRADED	MULLIONED	FREE SPACE	CONNOISSEUR	ABHOR
AVAILED	ENDEAVOR	INDUCE	BOURGEOIS	DELUGE
HEIR	CATASTROPHE	FINESSE	SKEIN	INERT

Hound of the Baskervilles Vocabulary

VIGIL	INCESSANT	PUGNACIOUS	AUSTERE	DISMAY
FIEND	SOLICITATIONS	SILHOUETTED	AGAPE	VEXATION
INEXORABLY	MALIGNANCY	FREE SPACE	UNMITIGATED	VILE
INDELIBLY	BRUSQUELY	INJUNCTIONS	MELANCHOLY	AMPLE
LUMINOUS	CLANDESTINE	FURTIVE	CORROBORATED	CIRCUMSPECT

Hound of the Baskervilles Vocabulary

INCESSANT	COMMUTATION	ABHOR	IMPLICIT	CIRCUMSPECT
MALIGNANCY	AUSTERE	CLANDESTINE	SILHOUETTED	AVAILED
PUGNACIOUS	MELANCHOLY	FREE SPACE	CONNOISSEUR	FIEND
MULLIONED	BALUSTRADED	CORROBORATED	VIGIL	PRESUME
BOURGEOIS	INEXORABLY	VILE	EXECUTOR	AMID

Hound of the Baskervilles Vocabulary

TENACITY	EQUESTRIAN	SKEIN	INDELIBLY	ENDEAVOR
FINESSE	FURTIVE	AUDACIOUS	INDUCE	SPECTRAL
VEXATION	BRUSQUELY	FREE SPACE	CATASTROPHE	INERT
APPROBATION	AGAPE	SOLICITATIONS	HEIR	DISMAY
DELUGE	UNMITIGATED	ERRONEOUS	LUMINOUS	APPARITION

Hound of the Baskervilles Vocabulary

ENDEAVOR	VILE	AMPLE	INERT	AUSTERE
VEXATION	INEXORABLY	CATASTROPHE	UNMITIGATED	MULLIONED
DISMAY	CIRCUMSPECT	FREE SPACE	FIEND	SPECTRAL
FINESSE	MALIGNANCY	ERRONEOUS	FURTIVE	INJUNCTIONS
BRUSQUELY	CONNOISSEUR	LUMINOUS	CORROBORATED	SKEIN

Hound of the Baskervilles Vocabulary

BALUSTRADED	PUGNACIOUS	AGAPE	TENACITY	ABHOR
AUDACIOUS	APPROBATION	CLANDESTINE	VIGIL	EQUESTRIAN
AMID	MELANCHOLY	FREE SPACE	INCESSANT	INDELIBLY
HEIR	AVAILED	BOURGEOIS	EXECUTOR	DELUGE
SOLICITATIONS	INDUCE	IMPLICIT	PRESUME	SILHOUETTED

www.ingramcontent.com/pod-product-compliance
Lightning Source LLC
LaVergne TN
LVHW081538060526
838200LV00048B/2131